Wagner Writes from Paris . . .

Portrait of the young Wagner by Ernst Kietz.

Wagner Writes from Paris . . .

*Stories, Essays and Articles
by the Young Composer*

Edited and Translated by
Robert L. Jacobs and Geoffrey Skelton

THE JOHN DAY COMPANY
An Intext Publisher
NEW YORK

Indexed in:
Essay

The John Day Company, 257 Park Avenue South, New York, N.Y. 10010.

Printed in the United States of America.

Now you are going to Paris. . . . It occupied so important a place in the development of my relations with the outside world that, whenever I think of such things, I invariably find myself remembering my experiences there. . . . As the world now is, Paris forms the culminating point: all other cities are simply stations along the way. It is the heart of modern civilisation, drawing in the blood before sending it out again to the limbs. When I decided to become a famous opera composer, my good angel sent me straight to that heart: there I was at the source, and there I was able to grasp at once things which at the wayside stations would perhaps have taken me half a lifetime to learn. . . .

Letter from Richard Wagner
to King Ludwig II of Bavaria
18 July 1867

Contents

Introduction

Richard Wagner was twenty-six years old when, after a stormy voyage from Riga to London, he crossed the English Channel and landed at Boulogne in August 1839, accompanied by his wife Minna and by Robber, a Newfoundland dog. The impecunious provincial *Kapellmeister*, who spoke little French and had no salon accomplishments, was travelling to Paris partly to escape his creditors, but mainly because Paris at that time was the centre of musical Europe. To have a work produced in its opera houses—the Grand Opéra, dominated formerly by Rossini and now by Meyerbeer, or the Opéra comique, the home of French composers such as Boieldieu and Auber, but not entirely closed to foreign composers—was to gain access to the stages of the whole world, and not least to the many court opera houses in Germany, whose inveterate provincialism made them look with more respect on foreign than on home products.

Wagner's belief in his genius had not been shaken by the rejection of his first opera, *Die Feen*, nor by the fiasco of the single performance of his second, *Das Liebesverbot*, in Magdeburg. He was bringing to Paris the first two acts of *Rienzi*, which he had composed in the naive expectation that his score would be accepted by the Paris Opéra on its merits. In Boulogne he had the good fortune to meet Meyerbeer, who recognised the worth of his score, supplied him with a number of introductions and promised his help for the future. Thus the young man entered Paris in good heart to take up residence, together with Minna and the dog, in a little hotel near the Rue St Honoré, one of the city's less fashionable districts.

It was a materialistic, pleasure-loving Paris to which they came. Louis Philippe, the bourgeois king, was on the throne, and his ministers, Soult and Guizot, were temporarily pursuing liberal policies at home and peaceful ones abroad. But it was an uneasy calm. After all, Napoleon's downfall was no further away from the Parisians of that period than the end of the Second World War is from us today; the July Revolution of 1830 was a recent memory and there were already signs of the discontent that came to a head in the revolution of 1848. In his constant satirical references to revolution as a French summer activity Wagner was not straying very far from the truth.

Certainly, in their feverish search for pleasure and material comforts, the prosperous bourgeois Parisians had little time to spare for new ideas, and the young musician from Germany soon realised that he would get nowhere unless he was prepared to play according to the Parisians' own rules. Meyerbeer's letters of introduction might gain him interviews with the powerful, but no commissions ensued. Meyerbeer himself was absent from Paris during most of the two and a half years Wagner spent there. An introduction to the manager of the Théâtre de la Renaissance did indeed lead to the prospect of a production of *Das Liebesverbot*, but then the theatre went bankrupt. Even the opportunity to provide the music for a vaudeville at the Théâtre des Variétés fell through. Attempts to interest celebrities like Pauline Viardot and Lablache in songs composed to suit the French taste led to nothing. The only introduction of Meyerbeer's which led to anything was that to the music publisher Maurice Schlesinger, who provided the hopeful young composer with an abundance of musical hackwork—arrangements of Donizetti's *La Favorita* and Halévy's *La Reine de Chypre* and the like. For this Wagner was obliged to be thankful, reduced as he was to living from hand to mouth, borrowing from whomever he could, at one time pawning every expendable household object and even his wedding ring.

His immediate friends in Paris were as poor and uninfluential as himself. Anders was a middle-aged German who worked at the Bibliothèque nationale; Samuel Lehrs was a philologist whose profound scholarship was not matched by an ability to capitalise it; and Ernst Kietz was a painter who lost custom because he was unable to complete commissioned portraits in time. (That Kietz was nevertheless a capable artist is suggested by his drawing of the young Wagner, reprinted here as a frontispiece by kind permission of Frau Winifred Wagner.)

Among companions such as these Wagner and Minna lived a sort of *vie de Bohème*, staying in a succession of apartments which varied in quality according to the current state of their finances. But, however bad these were, Wagner always took care (helped by Minna, a careful and resourceful housewife) to keep up outward appearances. If not on equal terms, he was still coming into contact with the great and famous. He met Liszt, at that time the idol of Paris basking in his glory, and did not take to him at all (no doubt envy had something to do with that); Berlioz, whom he admired as a composer but found unapproachable as a man; and the German poet Heine, who was living in exile in Paris. It was from a book of Heine's that he took the idea for his *Flying Dutchman*; he also set Heine's popular poem 'The Two Grenadiers' to music; and—more important in the context of this book—it was Heine's witty and satirical style that he borrowed when he was given the opportunity of earning some additional money by writing articles for French and German periodicals.

Here again he was indebted to Maurice Schlesinger. As well as music, Schlesinger published the *Gazette musicale*, a journal of considerable standing. Wagner owed him fifty francs for the engraving of his setting of 'The Two Grenadiers', and at Schlesinger's suggestion wiped off the debt by contributing the article *German Music*. So in the summer of 1840 he launched out on his literary career.

At first he wrote only for the *Gazette musicale*, where he was published in translation; in 1841 and 1842 he went further afield and contributed regularly to the *Abendzeitung* in Dresden, also sending occasional pieces to Schumann's *Neue Zeitschrift für Musik* and Lewald's quarterly *Europa*.

It is evidence of the keenness of Wagner's ambition and the superabundance of his energy that, in spite of all the drudgery of music arranging, journalism and fruitless lobbying in the struggle for a living, he managed in the latter half of 1840 to complete *Rienzi* and in the summer of 1841, which he spent in the country outside Paris, to compose *The Flying Dutchman* in seven weeks. The only success he had in Paris with these works was to sell the scenario of *The Flying Dutchman* to the Opéra, where it was used as the basis of an opera by an obscure French composer named Pierre Dietsch.

Salvation came from Germany, where Dresden accepted *Rienzi* and Berlin *The Flying Dutchman*. In April 1842 Wagner returned to his homeland, his mind busily occupied with plans for *Tannhäuser* (the idea for which he largely owed to his friend in Paris, the philologist Samuel Lehrs). Minna went with him of course—but not Robber, their Newfoundland dog: unwilling to share their meagre Bohemian life, he had abandoned them for a more prosperous owner.

Wagner continued to write essays and articles throughout his life, but they are for the main part expositions of his musical and dramatic theories. Valuable and illuminating as they are, particularly in relation to his own work, they lack the quality of sheer readability. Not so these early Parisian pieces. As Ernest Newman so rightly says in his biography of the composer: 'He never wrote better than at this period of his life: his pen has a speed and a variety of rhythm that it lost in later years when the burden of thought in him was too great for his literary faculty to carry in comfort.' He is not yet concerned to theorise: he writes unpretentiously with an open mind and one gets more than a whiff of the personality that fascinated his friends in Paris and indeed throughout his life. How very human he is in his volubility, his volatility, his inconsistency, his exaggeration, his intolerance, his quick abusive anger! And yet how impressive and endearing: an impassioned idealist, a penetrating thinker, a shrewd observer, warm-hearted, courageous and brimming over with high spirits, poetry and humour.

It was in order to present *this* Wagner that we decided to extricate these pieces from the relative obscurity of their position in the first of the ten volumes of the composer's collected writings and to present them by themselves in a new translation. In fact, we have gone further. When Wagner published the first volume he omitted some of his early Parisian pieces, and we have included a few of these (*Traps for Unwary Germans in Paris,* reports from Paris). We have restored the cuts he made when preparing the collected works (his main motive being to remove some nice things he had once said about Meyerbeer) and arranged the pieces in our own order which, with one or two exceptions, is chronological. We have also eliminated Wagner's footnotes—the afterthoughts of an older, not necessarily wiser man—because our feeling is that these early pieces should be left free to make the sort of impact that they must have made on the readers of their time.

The most intimately revealing piece in the collection is undoubtedly the semi-autobiographical short story *Death in Paris*. Berlioz praised it in the *Journal des Débats* and showed it to Heine, who is reported to have said that E. T. A. Hoffmann (upon whom Wagner had modelled himself) could not have done it better. Bernard Shaw too must have been an admirer: the reader who knows his *Doctor s Dilemma* will not fail to notice the resemblance between the dying Dubedat's artistic credo and the last speech of Wagner's hero. *A Pilgrimage to Beethoven* was also praised by Berlioz. In his collected works Wagner presents this story as a reminiscence written by the hero of *Death in Paris*: it too contains some autobiographical elements. Wagner himself was of course only a boy when Beethoven died, but at the age of nineteen he made a journey to Vienna, and in this story he draws on his memories to provide local colour. It can be regarded as an act of homage to the composer who had been the idol of his boyhood and who now meant more to him than ever, deepened as he was by his sufferings in Paris and enlightened by the performances of Beethoven's works which he heard there.

A Pilgrimage to Beethoven is by far the best known of all these pieces because it contains the biographically important first hint of the future theory of music drama. Less familiar, though surely no less fascinating, are the prophetic hints of a different kind to be discerned in *The Artist and the Public* and *German Music*. In the former, which was drastically cut in the *Gazette musicale*, Wagner is baring his soul as he describes the agonies of a genius struggling in the toils of the Parisian rat-race, driven at times to sacrifice honesty and sup with the devil, giving himself this right because 'his sufferings have made him feel that truthfulness is his very soul'. Does not this point to the equivocal morality of the later Wagner, whose conviction of the purity of his intentions served as a constant justification for conduct which greatly upset other people? And in *German Music*, though Wagner was obviously gilding the lily in order to impress his Parisian readers, one can discern that fanatical faith in a *distinctively German*, deep and disinterested love of music which underlay his wholesale repudiation of the mercenary entertainment world and his later assertion that it was all the fault of the Jews.

A Happy Evening, on the other hand, could be taken as the very reverse of prophetic: in this piece Wagner reveals his stature as a thinker with a clarity which he afterwards seldom attained. His penetrating analysis of the relation between music and emotion can be seen (and indeed has been in Suzanne Langer's seminal book *Philosophy in a New Key*) as a classic statement of the humanist approach to music—and apart from that as a personal affirmation of the unique joy, transcending all suffering, that an artist feels in being what he is.

All the pieces so far mentioned appeared in the *Gazette musicale*—nearly all in 1840 and early in 1841. Our introductory piece, *Traps for Unwary Germans in Paris*, was written in the summer of 1841, by which time Wagner had abandoned all thought of succeeding in Paris and pinned his hopes on productions of *Rienzi* and *The Flying Dutchman* in Germany. Thus he could regard Paris more objectively, and in this article (which appeared in Lewald's *Europa*) he provides his readers with a light-hearted cautionary survey. Needless to say, it should not all be taken literally: the rueful references to naive idealistic Germans struggling to cope with wily and cynical Parisians are the work of a born writer turning his own experiences to entertaining account—for example, his embarrassment at being taken for an Englishman at Boulogne. (Wagner made a different sort of literary capital out of that incident in *A Pilgrimage to Beethoven*!)

Apart from *The Virtuoso and the Artist*, which appeared in the *Gazette musicale* in a mutilated translation (the editor being unable to stomach Wagner's rudeness to the celebrities of the Italian Opera and their adoring public), all the other pieces in our selection were written for the German press, and nearly all in the more hopeful later period. Presented chronologically, they make a lively and perceptive record of personalities and events in the Paris of 1841. The reports from Paris which Wagner sent to the *Abendzeitung* in Dresden were intended to do just that. The articles—*Le Freischutz* and *A First Night at the Opéra*—have a wider significance. Wagner's graphic account of the havoc wrought upon Weber's masterpiece fascinatingly foreshadows the Opéra's catastrophic production of *Tannhäuser* twenty years later. *A First Night at the Opéra* is the only piece that conveys something of the more positive side of that Hollywood-like institution. In the gusto and vividness of his account of the production of Halévy's latest grand opera one can sense the depth of Wagner's involvement with the genre which in his hands was to become music drama—and the powerful attraction of its fountain-head, which had drawn him all the way from Riga.

In order to leave the reader free to enjoy these pieces as Wagner wrote them we have chosen to cut nothing from those we have selected and to dispense in the text with all scholarly adjuncts. We trust, however, that any questions that might arise in the reader's mind will be answered by the information contained in this introduction and in the Index and Notes, which give details of the persons and works mentioned. We also append a chronological list of all Wagner's early writings in Paris.

Traps for Unwary
Germans in Paris

Go and ask those shops in the Palais Royal, gleaming in their silver and gold, their silk and gaslight, what they are there for; ask the gardens of the Tuileries with their elegant, well-kept paths; ask the Champs Elysées with its splendid carriages and its powdered coachmen; the boulevards with their rich mixture of bustle and extravagance; the balconies of the theatres with their ravishing toilets and breathtaking coiffures; the opera balls with their irresistible *grisettes* in satin bodices and their expensive *femmes entretenues* in exclusive black velvet dominoes; and finally, when summer comes, ask the chateaux, the parks, the gardens, the hermitages and all the other fine pastoral pleasures the Parisian so innocently enjoys; ask all these things what they are there for. Is it, you may enquire, simply to provoke yawns of boredom? They will first protest and then scoff. What a stupid question! And yet there is a whole race of people in whom all these marvellous things can produce nothing but the most profound ennui. They are the Germans who live in Paris.

It really is true. There is nothing more boring on this earth than to be a German in Paris. Being German is fine when you are at home, where there is *Gemütlichkeit*, Jean Paul and Bavarian beer; where you can spend hours disputing about Hegel's philosophy or Strauss's waltzes; where there are fashion journals in which you can read about the latest murders in Paris or the cheapest places to buy *Gros de Naples*; and, last but not least, where you can hear or sing all the good old and new songs in praise of Father Rhine. There is nothing like this to be found in Paris, and yet a huge number of Germans live here. How great must their boredom be!

But I am also inclined to believe, looking at the other side of the coin, that there is nothing that bores a Parisian so intensely as a German. The main feeling is that Germans in general are honest people, whom one can trust. And that is bad, for, if they are trustworthy, it follows that they must be stupid, and for Parisians a stupid person is an abomination. Anyone who finds it impossible to enter into the intrigues, into the delicious deceptions, the ingenious indignities which are second nature to them, must inevitably appear stupid in their eyes. For, as they see things, a person who does not know how to get what he wants, or is spineless enough to die of hunger, must have taken leave of his senses.

So you see what a dangerous virtue honesty is, and how unfortunate a person must be who happens, like it or not, to be burdened with it. Through the obstacle of this one single virtue the German finds himself cut off from everything that makes Paris brilliant and enviable. Happiness, riches, fame, pleasure—these are not for him. His place is in the dirty streets, among the ragged beggars. The grocer is probably the only one who will appreciate his virtue—enough, at any rate, to grant him a little credit. But only a little, for the grocer knows the unhappy possessor of this virtue will never rise to the position of being able to settle a large bill.

That is the worst of it: in Parisian eyes no rich man can be honest, and consequently they think every honest man must be poor. But in Paris poverty is the ultimate sin. So, since all Germans are thought to be poor, they must also be regarded as stupid and bad—or in other words sinful.

It is appalling, this curse that lies on us Germans. You may think yourself the richest man in the world, but, unless you can produce blatant proof of it, you will be mercilessly treated as a poor man. To this day I have been completely unable to convince the Parisians that I am quite well off, though I have a yearly income of some two hundred florins, which in Germany would enable me to maintain a household with a large number of hangers-on. But here it counts for exactly nothing, and gradually people are even beginning to stop feeling obliged to take me for an Englishman.

Now this is a very curious matter about which I must tell you more. As everybody knows, the Parisians are a very polite people:

they never say unpleasant things to your face, unless it concerns their money. Since, however they are convinced that to call a man German is the same as calling him stupid or bad—or in other words honest and poor—they imagine they can pay us no greater courtesy than to pretend to take us for Englishmen. The French hate the English of course, but that, as we all know, is a political hatred, affecting the nation *en masse*. In fact, every individual Frenchman loves every individual Englishman to distraction and overwhelms him with expressions of undying regard. And why? Because in his eyes every Englishman is a rich man, however poor that man may be in his own estimation. What greater compliment can a Frenchman therefore pay us Germans than to say, '*Pardon, monsieur, vous êtes Anglais?*'

Since countless Germans must have suffered from this wretched French habit, I feel it is only right to reveal what trouble it once caused me.

As ill luck would have it, I first put my foot on French soil at Boulogne. I had come from England—indeed from London, that city of costly experiences. Arriving in the land of the francs, with its twenty sous pieces, I breathed a sigh of relief to have left the odious country of pounds, shillings and pence behind me, for I had reckoned that in France I could live at least twice as cheaply. My calculations were based on the relationship of sous to pennies, of which there are only twelve in each proud shilling, whereas the more modest-looking franc contains as many as twenty sous. This, with the added advantage of centimes at the rate of one hundred to the franc, led me to conclude that I should be able to put aside a good share of my yearly income. Thus during the journey across by steamship my head was full of pleasant hopes, prospects and even plans. In the end I had worked out that in time I should even be able to buy myself one of those castles in southern France, in the vicinity of the Pyrenees, of which Prince Pückler has told us such pleasant and auspicious things—such as, for example, that one would need no more than two thousand francs yearly to live in them in the way they should be lived in. I had the impression that Prince Pückler himself, looking at things from his princely perspective, had thought this to be quite a lot, and I convinced myself that my centime reckoning would enable me to reduce it to a quarter—which would bring it completely within my reach. And then—oh, cruel French customs, to make such a mess of my glorious plans!

As soon as I entered the hotel, I was asked, '*Pardon, monsieur, vous êtes Anglais?*' The journey on the steamer and my Pyrenean castles in the air had so benumbed my senses that in that moment I really did not at once recall which country I belonged to. The fact that I was a German never so much as occurred to me. And since, during my long absence from my homeland, I had received no definite news whether the town of my birth still belonged to Saxony or was now a part of Prussia, I thought in my confusion that the shortest way of ending my inner conflict would be to answer with a quick '*Oui*'.

Unhappy steamship journey, which summoned to my mind intoxicating visions of a Pücklerian castle in the Pyrenees! Unholy visions, which induced such confusion in me when the Boulogne hotelkeeper asked me my nationality! Calamitous uncertainty about the flag now flying in my native city that led me into so unpatriotic a lie! Disastrous falsehood! Pernicious '*Oui*'! Between you, you have destroyed all my beautiful plans, based with such brash confidence on the integrity of my centime system.

Convinced that living was cheap in France, I spent two days at the hotel. An excellent *garçon* attended with exemplary willingness and deference to my needs. I attributed his devoted service to the respect he felt for my qualities as an Englishman, and that I was not wrong in my assumption became abundantly clear when he happened to overhear one of the conversations I frequently hold with myself. His behaviour towards me underwent a sudden change. Naturally I had spoken to myself in German, and the *garçon*, who came from Geneva, recognised my true nationality at once. But what he withdrew from me in the way of respect and deference, the excellent man at once made good with unmistakable signs of fellowship. He became like a brother to me. He sat down at my table when he brought the coffee, helped himself to the sugar when he saw I did not want it and told me where I could go to buy tobacco when I asked him to fetch me some. However, a similar change of attitude had not, unfortunately, occurred in the gloomy mind of the hotelkeeper. It was clear to me, when he presented my bill, that he held

21

punctiliously to my '*Oui*'. In fact, he had even gone to the trouble of making the bill out in English. Certain bafflingly large sums contained in it led me to think they had got there by mistake, or at least had been intended for some other Englishman, presumably a real one. But the hotelkeeper helped dispel my doubts and bring me to a recognition of the truth. Everything was in order. My Pyrenean castle was gone beyond recall and—worse still—my touching faith in the infallibility of my centime system cruelly slain. I had to resign myself to the painful realisation that the prices on this bill were the same as in London, and sometimes even higher. And since here they were expressed in francs, of which there are more to the pound than shillings, the sight of them, even when the prices were the same as in London, was far more terrible.

Since this time I have always been careful to avoid answering the question, '*Pardon, monsieur, vous êtes Anglais?*' with an absent-minded '*Oui!*' Instead, I got myself into the habit of uttering a decided '*Non!*' and following it up immediately with a firm '*Allemand*'. This habit has brought me all the expected advantages, but on the other hand I have had to give up all hope of being treated with respect. When, under my true colours, I ask for a room, I am invariably shown to the fifth floor, and it takes all my powers of persuasion to induce the concierge even to show me a room on the fourth floor, let alone on the third. Waiters in restaurants, apprised of my German nationality, tactfully advise me against the more expensive dishes and, without asking, bring me sauerkraut or other good things which they consider most suitable for Germans.

Still, the situation also has its good side. Above all, the German's reputation for neediness saves him from offending against his own inborn morality: he is simply not in a position to keep mistresses. What this means in Paris will be clear to everyone who knows the city. Never mind what circles he moves in, a self-respecting man owes it to himself to keep a mistress. The workman, when he leaves his factory, the shop assistant, when he leaves his *magasin*, the student, when he leaves his college, goes, like any man of the highest standing, to meet his mistress. For it is the done thing and, were he not to do it, a workman, shop assistant or student would count for very little.

This excellent custom is naturally distasteful to Germans, and they have reason to be grateful that they are never likely to be troubled to the least degree in this regard. However large the number of fair creatures, however eager their search for accommodation, however inconstant their attachments, no *grisette* would ever for one moment consider forming a temporary alliance with a German. And much less would a German ever be so shameless or foolhardy as to seek such an alliance, for he would have to blush every time he caught sight of himself in a mirror, and there are a lot of mirrors in Paris. No, the Germans prefer to leave the business of mistresses to their fellow foreigners, the Britons. They are remarkably well adapted to it, and there is not one of them who has not within a day of his arrival formed a blissful, if fleeting relationship with a ballet dancer at the very least.

But it is precisely their lack of mistresses that cuts Germans so completely off from Parisian society. He is a stranger to all Parisian pleasures. There is no ball for him, no Chaumière, no Prado, no Tivoli; he shares no pastoral delights, no urban diversions. Paris goes about in pairs, male and female. Through their gay ranks, shyly watching their lively dancing, the German wanders like a sad hermit, bound by his involuntary oath of renunciation.

But how could it possibly be otherwise? However freely I have allowed my imagination to roam, I have never been able to visualise a German dancing the can-can. I have tried in all ways to provide my imagination with a feasible setting, racking my memory for the most frivolous figures and the most expressive faces that ever I encountered in Germany, granting them ten years of familiarity with the life and manners of Paris, yet never have I succeeded in envisaging a single one capable of successfully performing this graceful dance. The can-can is a fable with a moral that no German can understand, a riddle with a solution that no German ever hits upon. Once, now I come to think of it, I did see one of my countrymen, a very rash fellow, make an attempt to join the dance. It was a calamitous failure, for he appeared to be dancing a minuet.

All this may to some extent explain why the women of Paris seem to recognise in Germans the qualities they seek in genuine husbands. There are classes of society in which the domestic virtues are highly prized, and proper marriage contracts have a greater value than passing flights of fancy. What these circles appreciate is the man who stays at home, who opens and closes cupboards, who goes down into cellars, lights fires, carries children during the Sunday walk and fastens the hooks of his wife's dress. In such a man a high degree of faithfulness is hoped for, but the really desirable qualities are placidity, love and honesty. And of these honesty is the most important: it is exclusively on account of this virtue that German men are chosen for marriage, particularly by the widows of *marchands de vin*, tobacconists and *estaminet* owners.

These widows—of whom, incidentally, there are a great many about—have usually brought their late husbands some small dowry, which afterwards both parties have carefully invested, and it is therefore quite natural that the survivor (who is almost always the widow, for it is very rare for a man to outlive his first wife, unless he has struck her dead in a fit of temper, which can happen, as we know)—it is quite natural, I repeat, that the survivor should have no particular desire, after the death of her dearly beloved, to present the dowry and its earnings to someone else. She is far more interested in adding to it, if possible. From now on the widow is fighting for her own exclusive property, for hearth and shrine, and she has no intention of going shares again with another.

However, this raises certain difficulties. The lady is still in the best years of her life, she has any amount of energy left for the books and the correspondence, she knows exactly how much money is in the till. Enthroned behind her counter, she exudes an unmistakable majesty. But, be that as it may, she still needs a male creature around to raise and lower the shutters, to visit the cellar, to pour out the drinks—in a word, to perform the duties of a *garçon*. Why should she not, then, engage a *garçon*? There is an understandable drawback: *garçons* are not exactly renowned for their honesty. And then there are all the other things to be done—things to which no *garçon* would ever in his life consent. Who will look after the children? Who will do the shopping? Who will take the lady for a walk at four o'clock on a Sunday afternoon? And who will make life pleasant for her generally—since the widow, for all her excellent qualities, is still tender-hearted? Her dead husband did all these things. They are things that only a husband can be asked to do. So there is no help for it but to take another husband.

The widow is, however, still mainly concerned to preserve her exclusive rights over her property. Where is a man to be found who will take on all the immense duties of a husband without also claiming a share of the fortune? No Frenchman would consider the idea even for a moment and, if he did, it would only be because he hoped to trick the lady in spite of all her watchfulness.

And so at this point the widow is obliged to forget her national prejudices. Knowing as she does that in the veins of no people on earth does the blood flow more honestly and modestly than in those of the Germans, she hesitates no longer, but decides to bestow good fortune on one of our fellow-countrymen. Not only can he bring her everything she needs, but he also has the additional advantage of costing very little to keep, and on top of that, with his ambiguous accent, he will be able to entertain her with a flow of puns and comic expressions which, however uninventive he might ordinarily be, will fall daily from his lips.

This state of matrimony is, for many a German in Paris, the culminating point of much anxious effort and disappointed ambition. It is the harbour into which he steers his leaking, storm-tossed ship, pathetically resigned to making no further voyages of discovery. The vow he utters before the *maire* is the same vow of renunciation which pious souls, battered by the world's cruelty, formerly spoke as they took leave of the world to seek protection and salvation behind peaceful monastery walls.

In this way there has arisen in Paris a silent community in which the brothers, freed from the turmoils of strenuous passion, quietly dedicate themselves to the task of strictly observing the rules of their order. They feel no lash—except occasionally the lash of their wives' tongues—and they are absolved from chastity—at any rate towards their wives. But other joys are strictly forbidden. They are pledged to the education of the young, to the feeding of babies (through bottles, naturally), to the preservation of cleanliness in the matter of diapers, as well as to complete abstinence from any contact with silver and copper coins. Their nourishment consists of a *pot-au-feu* in the mornings, and in the evenings—as a special concession to their nationality—a dish of sauerkraut, for it is one of our misfortunes that the French imagine we Germans keep ourselves alive on nothing but sauerkraut.

No one ever leaves this order, except on the death of his other half. Since at the time the vow is taken these ladies are getting on in years, while the sacrificial victims of German honesty are usually young, it might be expected in the normal course of events that the latter would outlive their stern guardians. But these matrons have an enormously tenacious hold on life, and their captives never see the world again.

Who can know what remarkable individuals may be contained within this order? Might we not already have received a glass of *eau de vie* from the hands of a knowledgeable student of Hegel's philosophy? Might not the author of a five-act drama in verse have handed us two sous-worth of tobacco? Might not that pint of Strasbourg ale have been poured out for us by the most sensitive contrapuntalist in Kirnberger's school? The mind boggles at the inexhaustible range of possibilities. Who can conceive of all the sacrifices made by these unfortunates in order to live? Who can imagine what they had to renounce in order to gain admittance to that community?

I have followed the fate of one such German in Paris through all its stages. It is a short story, for, like everything else in this city, it happened very quickly and was all over in less than six months. He was a young man who had been brought to Paris by God knows what grievous trick of fate. His range of knowledge was unusually wide: he was a doctor, a lawyer, a writer, a poet and a scholar. He understood all of Goethe's *Faust*, from the Prologue in Heaven to the Chorus Mysticus at the end. He could write prescriptions and conduct lawsuits as well as any man. On top of that he could copy music, and produce proof that men have no souls. With all this enormous fund of knowledge and skill behind him, he naturally thought it would be easy enough, even if he started without a sou in his pocket, to make a respectable career in Paris, particularly since he was reckoning on the preparations for war that France had begun the previous autumn. These would undoubtedly provide an outlet for one of his talents at least. He was full of confidence when he visited me for the first time, even though he was well aware that Guizot's peace-loving policies might still put a spoke in his wheel.

A week later I received a letter from the Hotel Dieu hospital. My knowledgeable countryman had fallen ill and was taking advantage of the Parisians' friendly charity. Visiting him in this excellent establishment, I found him busy with a French grammar, striving to gain some knowledge of the language. His spirits were now somewhat lower than they had been, but all the same he had a multitude of plans in his head, all concerned for the time being only with the means of protecting himself from the possible ravages of hunger. Among other things he mentioned proof-reading for a printer, picture colouring, sticking covers on matchboxes—but what his heart was most set on was the possibility of singing in the chorus of the Grand Opéra (for my versatile fellow countryman could also sing). I promised to do what I could to help him, and gave him a supply of snuff.

Soon afterwards I received another letter—this time, however, from the Pitié hospital. I visited him there and had occasion to observe that this hospital was far meaner and less cleanly equipped than the Hotel Dieu. I was not clear why my judicious friend had changed his hospital, but I was relieved to find him in reasonably good health. I learned from him that nothing had so far come of his chorus singing, his matchbox covering, his colouring or his proof-reading; but on the other hand he was engaged on working out a proof that the soul was composed of carbonic acid and galvanism, and he hoped soon to be clear of his troubles.

And then came 15 December, the day on which Napoleon's ashes were brought to Paris. As everyone knows, God chose on this day to present the Parisians with appallingly cold weather. I stood freezing for four hours on a raised stand in the Place des Invalides and thought with envy of my friend, whom I imagined to be wrapped in the warm blankets of the Pitié. But the unhappy man had not been able to resist his urge for historical research (for he was also a historian), and he had decided to observe with his own eyes the laying to rest of the imperial remains in Paris. It was perhaps just as well, for otherwise he might easily have felt impelled to deny the reality of this burial in the same way that he denied the existence of the soul. All the same, the clothing the poor man wore was never designed for the cold of that remarkable day. It had obviously been made during one of its owner's happy past summers, and now it resolutely refused to provide adequate covering for the imposing limbs of my normally so prudent friend. His pitiful appearance cut me to the heart, and I felt that action must now be taken to meet the most pressing of his needs. I succeeded in finding an outlet for one of the very least of his accomplishments: the philosopher, lawyer, doctor and historian was obliged to copy music.

Soon, however, this method of breadwinning came to an end, for unfortunately I did not know a great number of people who had music to be copied. Something else had to be thought of. It was some days before I saw my soul-denying friend again, but he turned up unexpectedly in my room at last and informed me that he had very good prospects of securing a job as a sort of bookkeeper in a factory in Beauvais. The handsome salary involved would enable him in a very short time to save up a small capital, on which he could live without difficulty while carrying out the project that meant most to him. This was to explain Goethe's *Faust* to the French. The necessary knowledge of the French language which he would require for this undertaking he could easily acquire through his conversations with the factory workers.

Shortly afterwards he came to say goodbye, and I congratulated him and wished him every success. But when I asked him if he would be returning to Paris now and again, he told me that this would be difficult, since he was considering going to Australia. The Beauvais prospect had failed to materialise, but, in his capacity as doctor, he now had a good chance of securing a position on a ship carrying emigrants from London to Australia. He was expecting the money for his journey to London to arrive that very day. My farewell this time was very emotional, for a voyage to Australia is no joke. But soon I was to learn that my tears had been unnecessary: the money from London never arrived.

My unfortunate friend was now at a loss what to do. He had no money left, and I could not imagine how he managed to sustain himself. I had already noticed that he needed vast quantities of food to satisfy the demands of his extraordinarily robust constitution. I recalled how this need had once before clouded the usual equity and clarity of his judgment: speaking of the diet in Paris hospitals, he had maintained that it was designed to ruin the patients—the weak did not get enough nourishment to restore their strength, while the strong had no prospect but to become weak.

Through enquiries I at length discovered that two well-to-do ladies of the millinery trade had come to the rescue, attracted to him in the first place by the not unpleasing proportions of his figure. Their interest took the form, in the one case, of providing him with food and drink, and, in the other, of lending him twenty sous pieces. I cannot say for certain whether it was due to the fickleness of the charitable ladies or to a sense of shame in my otherwise so well-mannered friend that this arrangement very soon came to an end, but I do know that I one day found him struggling with problems of a very different kind. He told me that the widow of the deceased owner of an *estaminet* in a side street off the Rue St Antoine had been impressed by his qualifications as a husband. His needy circumstances had already led him, as he went on to declare, to start negotiations with the lady on the conditions underlying the prospective marriage bond. She had agreed to grant him board and lodging of an appropriate standard, together with all other rights and titles of a husband, excepting a claim on her property. In return he would be obliged to devote his full attention to the running of the establishment. And it was this point that my ambitious friend was utterly unwilling to accept. He had agreed to assume the full duties of the husband of an *estaminet* owner from midday to the small hours of the night, but he insisted on complete freedom during the morning hours, so that he could work on his interpretation of *Faust* and his proofs for the non-existence of the soul. In reply to this the lady had repeatedly insisted that the morning hours were the most profitable ones for the *estaminet*: he would have to serve the *pot-au-feu* and let both *Faust* and soul go hang. The inner struggle between material comfort and the consciousness of a higher calling was hard, but it ended nobly. With a heavy sigh my friend decided to renounce the prospect of a sheltered married life on the corner of the Rue St Antoine.

His reward soon came in the shape of a chance to become a sort of warder in a lunatic asylum. My friend was delighted, not only for the living it would provide, but also because it would be of great help in the researches on which he was currently engaged. God knows what the lunatics had against him, but here too he was obliged in the end to withdraw. He cast another glance in the direction of the *estaminet* widow, but decided it would be better to colour wrappings for sweets or publish a German periodical. Both projects fell through, and yet again the marriage battle arose in that tortured soul whose existence he denied. But he was able to put it all definitely behind him when a most favourable opportunity arose—a position as private tutor to the children of a famous and scholarly Englishman. Besides his riches and his children this Englishman also had leanings towards historical research, and since, as we know, my versatile friend was also a historian, what better position could he ever have hoped for? And this time fortune really did seem to be smiling on him. The Briton recognised the candidate's enormous worth—and engaged him.

For some time I did not see my lucky friend again, but, since I knew the Englishman intended to travel, it seemed quite natural to assume that his private tutor had gone with him. One day, when I was in the Jardin des Plantes admiring the bear cubs that had only just come into the world, I heard a child making an unbearable din just beside me. I looked around. Who shall describe my amazement when I saw this ill-behaved child—a boy of about four years of age—in the arms of my annotator of *Faust*? Respectably dressed, he was standing beside a matronly lady who held a large knitting bag in one hand and a little girl in the other. My friend looked momentarily startled, then, with an embarrassed smile, greeted me and invited me to visit him in his wife's *estaminet* on the corner of the Rue St Antoine. . . .

Poor France, who is going to explain Goethe's *Faust* to you now? Erring mortals, who will show you that your souls do not exist? The one man who could most clearly have done both now has his hands full serving *pot-au-feu* and Strasbourg beer!

This story contains material enough for ten years of residence in Germany. In Paris it all happened, as I said, within the space of six months. It could indeed have been completed in yet shorter time if my knowledgeable friend had gone about solving his difficulties more forcefully, if he had been prepared to resort to cunning or forbidden methods of some sort—in a word, if he had considered following the Parisian system of intrigue and fraud. But all the ingenious dodges with which a German at home manages to maintain a creditable reputation, often for years on end, are of little use in Paris. All of them are mere child's play in comparison with the consummate artistry of the Paris sharper. I recall with regret another fellow-countryman of mine who—probably less because he thought it right than because he thought it expedient—tried to make his living through petty frauds and innocuous evasions of the Paris laws. I believe he soon found out that the lawless Parisians have laws against everything—and especially against German inspirations. This man did not stay very long in Paris.

It really does seem as if, for any poor German devil who wants to get on in Paris, inventive talent is the least valuable of his qualifications. A talent for music is much more promising. With music the Germans have amassed so much credit that no Frenchman can even conceive of a German who does not understand it. If it should happen at a party that there is no pianist at hand to accompany a ballade by Demoiselle Puget, and it is learnt that a German is present, then everyone breathes again. For what reason could this German have been begotten by his father and born of his mother if not to play the piano? Should it however turn out that the German, through too much study of Hegel's philosophy, has neglected to recognise and develop his musical talents, and should he therefore be obliged to decline the invitation of a Parisian lady to accompany her in a Puget ballade, then this lady will hasten to cross herself, for what can that German be but a ghost, a phantom, a monster? However, if the German understands music and can play the piano, he can look forward with confidence to a brilliant career. He can become a virtuoso or a teacher—in fact anything he wants to be except a minister, as Spontini became in our country. And he can do something even better than that: he can marry the daughter of a banker, for even in the higher classes of society a certain sympathy exists for German marriages, especially if it is the outcome of a mutual passion for art—which nobody is more adept at stimulating than a German seated at a piano. But here of course his career as a musician ends. Further than to be the son-in-law of a banker he cannot go—at least not by virtue of what he is or what he does. If he does ascend from here to higher spheres of fortune—if, for example, he becomes the statutory composer of the Grand Opéra, like Meyerbeer—this he will achieve only through being a banker in his own right. In Paris a banker can do anything—even compose operas and have them put on.

Thus it would be reasonable to conclude that the best way for a German to get on in Paris is to be a banker. But German bankers, of whom there are a considerable number here, no longer count as Germans. They are above nationality, and so immune from all national prejudices: they belong to the universe and the Paris Stock Exchange. However well endowed with stocks and consols these bankers may be, they do nothing to shake the French conviction that all Germans are by definition poor, since it would never occur to anybody to think of them as Germans. At the most a Parisian might discriminate to the extent of saying, when talking of a German banker, '*Ce monsieur est banquier, je crois Allemand*'; whereas of a German author he would say, '*Il est Allemand, je crois homme de lettres.*' In their eyes Rothschild is a universal Jew rather than a German. Even his German name is seldom spoken aloud—usually he is referred to as 'No. 15, Rue Lafitte'.

It is also the German bankers' own primary concern, once their business is more or less established, to divest themselves of their German nationality. They try to be more French even than the French, and in fact they are the only ones who manage to imitate French manners so that one can scarcely tell the difference. They succeed very well in aping the Parisians' egoism, but less well when they seek to imitate their refined behaviour: there are German bankers, it is said, who can, if roused, be as coarse as any German police official. As a rule they tend to become acutely embarrassed if addressed in their native language. Shame brings a gleam to their eyes and a modest flush to their yellow cheeks, for every German banker, be he never so fat, retains in private life, and when he is speaking French, a dull eye and a pale cheek. All this makes them popular—and is accordingly good for business

The best and truest Germans are the poor ones. In Paris they learn all over again to appreciate their native language, and this makes them forget to learn French. Their failing sense of patriotism is given new life and, however reluctant they may be to return to their home-land, they grow ill with homesickness. They need a full year to accustom themselves to Paris, and till then they look askance at every street urchin and every picture shop. They soon learn to avoid the urchins, but the picture shops they come to love and honour. Many spend hours at them every day, for there they can study Paris and learn something about its inhabitants. In these shops they can find out what is happening both in public and in private life, for almost daily there are new pictures and caricatures to look at, and through these they discover the secret of the city's social and political significance. When two Germans meet, it is quite natural that they should exchange experiences, and very often these are simply things seen and heard at the picture shops. They declare that they saw two children standing in front of a picture of Adam and Eve and heard one ask which was the man and which the woman. 'You can't tell,' the other replied, 'because they've got no clothes on.' Or they might go on to tell of a grocer they saw returning from service in the national guard. He discovered his wife trying to conceal her lover. The grocer drew his sword and was about to run the lover through when his wife threw herself at his feet with the cry, 'Unhappy man, would you kill the father of your children?' Experiences of this sort can be had every day at the picture shops. The Germans appropriate them and are convinced it all happened before their very eyes.

Most of these poor Germans have plenty of imagination and talent, but above all they are loyal friends: speaking for myself, it was here I first learned the true meaning of friendship. They also form a silent community in Paris, and they too have taken a vow of self-denial: they live chastely and meticulously observe the country's laws. All the same, they do often hanker after conquest, and bold plans and desires not infrequently trouble their hearts. For who could possibly remain indifferent when, having paid four francs at the box-office of the Opéra, he takes possession of a seat on one of the red velvet benches in the pit? Before him he sees the slimmest and most elegant ballerinas in the world, stretching longing feet towards the Jockey Club box, where their lovers are sitting. Beside him, at a higher level, he is conscious of gracious ladies with dazzling necks and enchanting costumes, radiating perfumes intoxicating to a nose accustomed to the stink of gas. Behind him he sees a mysterious illuminated box, above which are inscribed the awe-inspiring initials L.P. These stand for Louis Philippe, but are sometimes erroneously taken to mean Léon Pillet, the opera house's director. The whole forms an ensemble which could really tempt the poor German brotherhood to forget its vows. Probably no one would go so far as to break them—who has the strength or the means to do so? —but frivolous thoughts cannot always be suppressed.

Such vain thoughts usually lead to a state of the most violent ennui. When that happens, all the arts of Liszt and Chopin, all the tones of Duprez and Dorus-Gras, even Rubini's imperishable trills are rarely able to dispel feelings of boredom; on the contrary, they all too frequently only succeed in adding to them.

Happy days, then, when spring comes round and gives one a reason to flee from this incorrigible Paris with its awful temptations and wearisome relaxations. For at that time of year there is nothing in Paris for Germans to do, except at best to look at the giraffes or wait for a revolution. The Parisians themselves have a thousand and one other things to keep them busy, even in the summer. But the German, emerging from the hard deprivations of winter, longs for only one thing—the still delights of the countryside.

But what countryside can you find in Paris? The city has a circumference of at least forty German miles. Wherever you go, there are bankers' residences and houses full of ministers and plutocrats.

So it was with feelings of true bliss that I came on a house, built in ramshackle style, standing all by itself at a spot five miles outside Paris. How my heart jumped for joy at the prospect of being alone, without neighbours—a pleasure which one can learn to appreciate only in Paris. Taking a room in this building, I was further delighted to discover, from the mass of pictures I could see in his quarters, that the owner was a painter. True, they were terrible pictures, but they gave me the comforting assurance that my landlord's trade was at least a silent one. There is nothing disturbing about pictures, as long as one does not have to look at them.

I was amused by my landlord's strikingly original appearance. He was some eighty years old, but he had the vigour of a man of forty. He told me he had spent a large part of his life at the court of Versailles. He was therefore a Legitimist, and all the more so since the July Revolution had robbed him of a pension of one thousand francs. I expressed my sympathy with him and gave him my reasons for considering the Legitimist cause an excellent one. This pleased him very much, but also added to his disappointment at my apparent indifference to Legitimist affairs when once, in a fit of absentmindedness, I deeply offended him. He had been telling me that he could still vividly remember the funeral of King Louis XV's consort, and I asked him: did he mean Madame de Pompadour or Madame Dubarry?

However, on the first day we remained good friends. The only thing that disturbed me was the sight, when I looked out of my window, of a bath tub standing out in the open in the middle of the back garden. My Legitimist friend had the habit of filling this with water in the morning, leaving it to be warmed by the sun and then getting into it, in highly illegitimate undress, before dinner.

But this worthy favourite of Madame Dubarry—for such he had been—still had another and far more disturbing surprise in store for me. I had not seen all the other rooms in his house and was thus unaware of the big collection of musical instruments which he kept in one of them. The wretched man had another hobby besides painting and Legitimist politics—and that was the invention of new implements for transmitting sound, which he tried out one after another every evening and every morning. You can imagine what I suffered from this cruel habit of my landlord's when I assure you that, in spite of all my efforts, I have not to this day succeeded in guiding his dreadful inventive urge into other and quieter channels.

No, it is simply not possible to find refuge in solitude from the emanations of Parisian culture without making a long journey. Happy is the banker who can afford such journeys. Happy too the native Parisian, who needs no such respite! But to the Germans of Paris who are not bankers my heart goes out. They will be submerged in this sea of unenjoyable enjoyment for ever, if they do not succeed in becoming bankers.

So to all you thirty thousand German nationals in Paris I can only wish a happy release!

German Music

Thanks to the endeavours of a number of excellent artists who seem to have banded together for that very purpose, the masterpieces of German music are no longer unknown to the Parisian public. They have been performed in the worthiest manner and received with the greatest enthusiasm. So the barriers, which no doubt will always divide nations themselves, but which should never be allowed to divide their arts, are beginning to be destroyed. Indeed one may assert that open-hearted recognition of foreign works is a distinguishing feature of the French rather than of the Germans, and this though the latter, one might almost say, weakly subject themselves to every foreign influence with more alacrity than is good for the maintenance of their own independence. The difference is this. Being as he is unable to establish a mode of his own, the German unthinkingly adopts one from abroad; in his weakness he forgets his own identity and blindly sacrifices his own judgment to the foreign influence. However, this applies principally only to the mass of the German public. For on the other hand we have the professional musician who, perhaps out of disgust at the general weakness, divides himself too sharply from the mass and in a spirit of false patriotism adopts a one-sided, unfair attitude to foreign products. With the French it is the other way round: the mass of the public is perfectly satisfied with the national product and feels not the slightest desire to broaden its taste. All the more whole-heartedly therefore do the higher classes of music-lover acknowledge foreign merit; they love to admire and applaud things beautiful and unknown from abroad. As witness the enthusiastic reception which has been so quickly accorded to German instrumental music. Though, apart from this, whether one could say that the French completely *understand* German music is another question, the answer to which must be doubtful. Certainly it would be wrong to maintain that the enthusiasm evoked by the Conservatoire orchestra's masterly performance of a Beethoven symphony is affected. Yet when one listens to this or that enthusiast airing the various opinions, ideas and conceits which such a symphony has suggested to him one realises at once that the German genius is still very far from being completely grasped. . . . Let us therefore take a comprehensive look at Germany and the state of her music in order to indicate more clearly how it should be understood.

It has been said that whereas the Italians use music for love-making and the French for social reasons, the Germans cultivate it as a form of science. It would be better perhaps to say that the Italian is a singer, the Frenchman a virtuoso and the German—a musician. The German has the right to be dubbed simply a 'musician' because it can be said of him that he loves music for its own sake— to him it is not a means of charming or of earning money and a reputation, but a divine art which he worships and which when he abandons himself to it means everything in the world to him. The German is capable of writing music solely for himself and his friends without any thought of its ever being performed in public. The longing to make a brilliant success seldom seizes him since most Germans have no idea how such a thing could be done. Before what public should he appear? His fatherland is divided into a number of kingdoms, electorates, duchies and imperial free cities. He lives, say, in the main centre of a duchy where, there being no public, it does not enter his head to shine. If he is really ambitious or if he is compelled to earn his living by music he goes to the ducal palace. But in that small palace there are already plenty of good musicians. He has a very hard time of it making his way, but in the end he pulls through and his music is liked. But in the neighbouring duchy not a soul has ever heard of him. How then can he possibly make a name for himself in Germany? He tries to, grows old in the attempt and dies; he is buried and nobody ever mentions him again. This is roughly the fate of hundreds; can it be wondered then that thousands never so much as consider making a career out of music? They prefer to take up some craft in order to support themselves and be able to devote their spare time all the more undisturbed to music—not in order to shine, but to be refreshed and ennobled thereby. But let it not be thought that the music they make is merely craftsmanlike! Oh no! Go and listen to them playing in a little room on a winter evening. A father and his three sons are seated round a table; two of the sons play the violin, the third the viola, the father the cello. The piece they are playing with such understanding and fervour is a quartet composed by that little fellow who is beating time. He is a schoolmaster from the neighbouring village, and this quartet of his is finely wrought, beautiful and deeply felt. Go to that place, I say, and listen to the music of that composer and it will so touch you that you will be moved to tears; you will discover what German music is, you will feel the German spirit! No brilliant passages here for this or that virtuoso to bring down the house with; all is pure and innocent, and for that very reason noble and elevated. But put these splendid musicians before a large audience in a brilliant salon and they will no longer be the same. They will be too shy even to raise their eyes. They will be afraid that they will be unable to satisfy your standards. They will enquire what kind of musical arts you are accustomed to and then in their stupid lack of self-confidence shamefully deny their own nature in a hasty endeavour to imitate those arts which they only know from hearsay. They will nervously prepare to regale you with brilliant passages: those same voices which sang a beautiful German song so movingly now hurriedly practise Italian coloratura. But their passages and their coloratura do not come off; you have heard far better; you have no patience with these duffers. And yet those duffers are the truest artists; their hearts glow with a finer warmth than was ever radiated by those who delight you in your brilliant salons. What went wrong with those artists? They were too modest; they were ashamed to be true to themselves. That is the sad side of the history of German music.

Severe barriers are imposed upon the German musician on the one hand by nature, on the other by the political structure of his fatherland. Nature denies him that easy supple mastery of the voice which fortunate Italian throats have; the political structure makes it difficult for him to reach a wide public. The opera composer is compelled to learn from the Italians how to write for the voice, while for his works themselves he has to seek a stage abroad since there is none in Germany upon which he can present himself to the nation as a whole. Regarding this last point, one can assume that the composer who brings out his works in Berlin is for that very reason completely unknown in Vienna or Munich: it is only from abroad that he can make his name known all over Germany. German works always have the character of a provincial product, and if to an artist even a great nation seems too small, how much smaller must one of its provinces appear in his eyes! An individual genius no doubt surmounts all these barriers, though thereby he is almost bound to sacrifice something of his national independence. In a certain sense the essential character of the German always remains provincial; thus we have Prussian, Swabian and Austrian folk-songs but no truly German one.

This lack of centralisation which explains why no great musical piece of nation-wide significance will ever appear is nevertheless also the reason why music among Germans has always preserved its character of inwardness and truth. Precisely because there is no great court which gathers to itself all Germany's artistic resources in order to harness them to the pursuit of a single attainable goal— precisely for this reason in every province artists are to be found who practise their beloved art independently. The consequence of this is a spreading of music all over the country, even to the most unlikely places, the humblest cottages. It is astonishing what musical resources one often finds alongside each other in the most insignificant German towns. Though singers for the opera may be scarce, everywhere one meets an orchestra which is usually able to give an excellent account of a symphony. In towns of from twenty to thirty thousand inhabitants one can reckon not merely upon one, but upon two or three well organised orchestras, not to mention innumerable amateurs who are often just as capable as the professionals, and sometimes even better trained. Furthermore one must bear in mind just what is meant when one speaks of a German musician. One rarely finds an ordinary orchestral player who plays only the instrument for which he is engaged; usually he plays at least three with equal facility. And what is more important, usually he is also a composer, and not a mere empiricist either, but thoroughly grounded in harmony and counterpoint. Most of the members of an orchestra playing a Beethoven symphony know it by heart—this knowledge of theirs indeed often gives rise to a certain arrogance which has a detrimental effect on the performance in that each musician concentrates upon his own individual conception regardless of the ensemble.

One can take it then that in Germany music has branched out to the humblest, unlikeliest places—indeed that perhaps it has its roots there. For in this connection the higher, more brilliant society in Germany can be regarded merely as an extension of those humble narrow circles. Let us assume then that it is among those quiet unpretentious families that German music feels truly at home—and indeed among those families, where music is regarded not as a medium for showing off, but as a spiritual refreshment, German music really is at home. Among those simple honest souls art, since it is not concerned to entertain a vast heterogeneous public, naturally sheds its gaudy coquettish trappings and reveals the charm of its essential qualities of purity and truth. Here it is not merely the ear that demands to be satisfied, but the heart and the soul that seek refreshment; the German wants not only to feel his music, but to think it. The desire for mere sensuous pleasure gives way to a longing for spiritual nourishment. Therefore, since it is not enough for the German merely to apprehend music sensuously, he acquaints himself with the art's inner organism. He studies it; he studies the theory of counterpoint in order to clarify his understanding of the masterpieces which attract him so powerfully and wonderfully. He learns the fundamentals of his art and ends by becoming a composer himself. This desire for learning is handed down from father to son and the obligation to satisfy it becomes an essential part of education. A German learns all the difficult part of musical theory in his childhood along with his school studies, with the result that when he reaches the stage of being able to think and feel for himself nothing is more natural than that music should be part of his thinking and feeling, and that far from regarding it as a mere entertainment he should approach it in a religious spirit as one of the holiest things in his life. He thus becomes a devotee—and the deep pious devotion which infuses his understanding and practice of the art is the thing which mainly characterises German music.

This habit of mind—and also perhaps the lack of fine voices—causes the Germans to direct themselves to instrumental music.

If it is true that in every art there is a genre which best represents its characteristic essence, then in the case of music that genre would certainly be instrumental music. Into every other genre a second element enters which (as we know from experience) by its very nature destroys the unity and independence of music without itself ever reaching the same height. Think of the chaotic mass of appendages from the other arts which have to be taken into consideration before we can grasp the real purpose of the music whenever we hear an opera! Think how the composer feels himself compelled here and there to subordinate his art completely, and moreover often for the sake of things which affront the dignity of art! In those fortunate cases where the contribution from the other arts is on the same high plane as the music a truly new genre is created, whose classic stature and deep significance have been sufficiently acknowledged. Even so this genre must always remain inferior to that of instrumental music because it involves a sacrifice of music's independence, whereas in instrumental works music attains its highest significance and is brought to its most perfect development. In this realm, free from every alien cramping influence, the artist is in a position to achieve the ideal of art in the most direct way; in this realm, where the resources he employs are peculiar to his art, he is indeed compelled to remain within its sphere.

Can it be wondered that it is to this genre above all others that the serious-minded and devoted German is attracted? Here, where he can give rein to his dreams and fantasies, where his imagination is not restricted to the expression of a single specific passion, where he can lose himself in the great realm of indefinite feeling—here he feels himself free and at home. To realise the masterpieces of this genre of art no brilliant stage is called for, no expensive foreign singers, no splendid theatrical production. A piano, a violin suffices to conjure up imaginative effects of overwhelming power and brilliance. Everybody plays one or the other, and the smallest community contains enough instrumentalists to form an orchestra of its own capable of rendering works on the grandest scale. Can the most sumptuous contribution from the other arts lead to the creation of a more magnificent edifice than a Beethoven symphony performed by a simple orchestra? Surely not! The most gorgeous trappings can never represent what a performance of these masterpieces sets forth as a living reality.

It comes to this, then, that instrumental music is the exclusive property of the German—it is his life, his creation! Perhaps that shy unassuming modesty which is a main feature of the German spirit has a great deal to do with it. This modesty prevents the German from making a display of his art, his private sacred possession. With a true sense of delicacy he feels that this would be tantamount to a denial of his art, that its nature is so eternally pure that it is easily disfigured by the pursuit of worldly splendour. His joy in music he cannot communicate to the masses, but only to an intimate circle. There he can let himself go. There his tears of joy and sorrow flow unrestrained, and so it is there that he becomes an artist in the fullest sense of the term. If the circle is very small then a piano and a couple of string instruments will serve—a sonata is played or a trio or quartet, or one sings a German four-part song. If the intimate circle widens that means there are more instruments and so one plays a symphony. . . . So one can picture instrumental music as an art which has grown out of the heart of German family life; as an art which cannot be understood and appreciated by a public but only by a small intimate circle. To experience the authentic lofty rapture known only to the initiated a certain pure noble quality of enthusiasm is demanded, and this is something which can only be felt by a true musician, not by a pleasure-seeking salon-audience. The latter, in that they follow and enjoy the music merely as a succession of piquant, brilliant episodes, totally misunderstand it: what springs from the inmost core of the purest art they treat merely as though it were yet another form of empty titillation.

It will now be my task to show how instrumental music is the basis of all German music.

I have already indicated why the German is by no means so much at home with vocal as he is with instrumental music. It cannot of course be denied that vocal music among the Germans has taken a specific direction of its own, whose point of departure is to be found both in the character and in the needs of the people. Nevertheless the greatest and most important branch of vocal music, namely dramatic music, has never reached the same height nor undergone the same independent development as instrumental music. German vocal music flourished in the churches; opera was left to the Italians. Not that Catholic church music has ever been at home in Germany; this can only be said of Protestant music. The reason for this is again the simplicity of the German way of life, to which the ecclesiastical splendour of Catholicism is far less suited than the modest unpretentious Protestant ritual. The pomp of the Catholic church service was taken over from foreign princes and courts, and more or less all German composers of Catholic church music have been imitators of the Italians. The older Protestant churches had no use for pomp, but were content with a simple chorale sung by the whole congregation and accompanied by an organ. This song, whose noble dignity and unembellished purity could only have been the product of a simple and genuine piety, must surely be regarded as an exclusively German heritage. And indeed its artistic structure has all the character of German art. The people's love of song is revealed in the brevity and popular style of the chorale melodies, some of which are strikingly similar to other secular—yet always naively pious—folk songs. And the rich and powerful harmonies to which the Germans set their chorale melodies reveal the nation's deep artistic intuition. The chorale then—in itself one of the most impressive phenomena in the history of art—must be regarded as the foundation of all Protestant church music. Artists built further upon it and constructed some magnificent edifices. The first great enlargement was the motet, a form of composition based on the same church songs as the chorale, but sung by voices alone without any organ accompaniment. The finest examples we possess are the motets of Johann Sebastian Bach who must be regarded as altogether the greatest of the composers of Protestant church music.

The motets of this master, which were used in the church service in the same way as the chorale (except that owing to their greater difficulty they were performed by a special choir instead of by the congregation) are unquestionably the most perfect unaccompanied music ever written. For all that they contain a wealth of artistic skill employed in the profoundest possible way, the ruling element is always the simple, powerful, often highly poetic treatment of the text in a genuinely Protestant sense. At the same time the perfection of their formal structure has a magnitude and self-sufficiency unsurpassed in the whole realm of art. But a still greater expansion of this genre is to be found in the great Passion music and in the oratorios. The Passion music is almost exclusively the creation of the great Johann Sebastian. Its basis is the story of the Crucifixion as narrated by the Evangelists; the whole text is set to music word by word; furthermore verses from church songs relating to specific portions of the narrative are introduced at appropriate moments; at the most important passages the chorales themselves are sung by the whole congregation. A performance of a Passion thus becomes a great religious festival in which musicians and congregation play an equal part. What a wealth of artistry these unique masterpieces have, what strength and clarity, and yet what unadorned purity! They embody the whole essence and substance of the German nation—the more so since, as I have sought to show, they stem from the hearts and customs of the people.

Church music then owed both its origin and its achievements to the fact that it met the needs of the people. No such need has ever been felt by Germans for dramatic music. Opera after its rise in Italy acquired a character of such sensuousness and splendour that the serious, sensitive German could not possibly have felt a need for the pleasure it offered. Garnished as it was with ballet and pompous decoration, it soon fell into disrepute as a mere luxurious court entertainment—indeed at first it was only as such that it was patronised and cultivated. Since courts, especially German ones, are completely separated and shut off their pleasures could of course never be the same as those of the people. Hence the fact that throughout nearly the whole of the last century opera in Germany was cultivated as a wholly foreign art-form. Every court had its Italian troupe, which sang operas by Italian composers, since at that time opera was only conceivable in the Italian language and sung by Italians. German composers who wanted to write operas had to learn the Italian language and mode of singing; to be favourably received they had to denationalise themselves completely as artists. Even so, in this genre, too, Germans often carried off the palm: the tendency towards universality, of which the German genius is capable, made it easy for them to make themselves at home on foreign soil. We know how rapidly Germans feel themselves into the inborn national character of their neighbours; thereby they provide themselves with a fresh standpoint from which their own genius is able to spread out and soar far above the limiting barriers of nationality. It is almost as though the German genius were destined to seek from its neighbours what it did not inherit from its motherland and to lift what it takes out of its narrow boundaries and provide something universal for the whole world. Naturally this can only be achieved by one who is not content merely to counterfeit a foreign nationality but who preserves pure and uncorrupted the endowment of his German birth, namely, genuineness of expression and purity of invention. When this heritage is preserved the German must achieve the highest in every language and in every country under the sun.

So we see at last that it was a German who lifted the Italian school of opera to an ideal perfection and presented it to his countrymen broadened and ennobled to the point of universality. This German, this supreme, divine genius, was Mozart. The history of all German art and of all German artists can be read in the story of the upbringing and of the life of this single German. His father was a musician; he was trained to become one probably only with the intention of making out of him an honest musician able to earn his daily bread. In early childhood he was made to learn the most difficult theoretical aspects of his art; thus in his boyhood he was already a complete master. Furthermore his tender child-like nature and the extreme delicacy of his ear made for the deepest possible assimilation of his art. But it was his colossal genius that raised him above all other masters of whatever art in any century. Even the external features of his life conform completely to the national pattern: he was poor and needy; he shyly rejected ostentation and worldly advancement. This artist, who was modest to the point of bashfulness and so lacking in ambition that he neglected his own interests, achieved the incredible, bequeathed to posterity treasures beyond reckoning without ever realising that he was doing more than obeying his impulse to create. In the whole history of art no life story is more moving and uplifting.

Mozart is the supreme example of that universality of which, as

45

I have said, the German genius is capable. He assimilated foreign art in order to elevate it to the realm of the universal. His operas were written in Italian since at that period this was the only acceptable language for singing. Yet, in that he cut out all the weaknesses of the Italian style and ennobled its best features by infusing them with his native German thoroughness and strength, he brought forth something entirely novel and unprecedented. This new creation of his was the most beautiful, the most ideal flowering of dramatic music—from this point onwards opera can be reckoned to have taken root in Germany. National theatres sprang up and operas began to be written in the German language.

While this great epoch was forming, while Mozart and his predecessors were creating a new genre out of Italian music, the music of the popular stage was undergoing a development; eventually the fusion of the two led to the creation of the true German opera. I refer to the German *Singspiel* whose roots lay far removed from the glitter of courts in the customs and nature of the people. This German *Singspiel* or operetta bears an unmistakable resemblance to the older French Opéra comique. Its subjects were drawn from the life of the people and most of them depicted the customs of the lower classes. They were usually comedies and full of an earthy natural wit. Vienna must be regarded as the principal home of the *Singspiel*: more than anywhere else national characteristics have been preserved in the imperial city, whose gay carefree inhabitants always respond most readily when their natural wit and light-hearted fantasy are appealed to. So it was in Vienna, where all popular pieces had their origin, that the popular *Singspiel* fared best. Composers confined themselves mainly to airs and ariettes; even so, among them one finds pieces of real character—for example, Johann Schenk's admirable *Dorfbarbier* —which, had they been built upon, would have in time increased the significance of the genre, had not its fusion with the greater operatic music led to its complete eclipse. Nevertheless the genre did attain a certain independent stature: it is a surprising fact that while Mozart's Italian operas immediately after their appearance were translated and presented to the entire German public, these operettas were enriching their form by employing subjects from folk-legends and fairy tales which most appealed to the imaginative Germans.

Then at last the decisive event took place: Mozart aligned himself with this national movement of the German operetta and made it the basis of the first great German opera: *The Magic Flute*. From the point of view of a German the importance of this work cannot be overestimated. Hitherto German opera had been virtually non-existent: with this work it was created. The librettist, a Viennese theatre director, was a speculator whose intention was simply to bring out a large scale operetta. Thus the work had all the appearance of being designed for popularity: it was based on a fantastic fairy tale and stocked with wonderful fairy-tale apparitions and a good dose of hearty comedy. What Mozart built upon the basis of this strange hotchpotch! The divine magic that pervades the whole work from the most popular song to the most solemn hymn! The versatility, the range! It is as though the quintessence of all the noblest flowers of art were united and blended in a single bloom. How unforced and yet how noble is the popular quality in every melody from the simplest to the mightiest! In point of fact the giant stride of the genius went almost too far: in creating the German opera Mozart brought forth a masterpiece of unsurpassable perfection, one indeed which ruled out any further continuation and expansion of its genre. German opera, it is true, lived on, but as it had risen rapidly to its greatest height so it deteriorated into shallow mannerism. In this sense Winter and Weigl must be regarded as Mozart's most direct imitators. Both whole-heartedly aligned themselves with the popular trend in German opera, and the latter in *Die Schweizerfamilie* and the former in *Das unterbrochene Opferfest* showed how well the German opera-composer appreciated the nature of his task. Nevertheless in the hands of his imitators the element of the universal in Mozart's treatment of the popular trend was lost sight of in trivialities; it became evident that German opera could never acquire a *national* status. The characteristic popular quality of the rhythms and melismata stiffened into embellishments and phrases of an insignificant stereotyped kind; above all, the utterly careless way in which composers chose their subjects revealed how ill-fitted they were to raise German opera to a higher level.

And yet a popular musical drama did once again arise. While Beethoven's mighty genius was opening up a new world of daring romanticism in his instrumental music, a light from that magic region shed its radiance upon German opera. Weber it was who breathed a fresh warm lovely life into the music of the stage. In *Der Freischütz*, his most popular work, he touched the heart of the German people. Here a German legend, a horrific saga, was brought by the poet and the composer directly to the people; its basis was the simple soulful German song, so that the whole was like a great moving ballade—a ballade decorated in the noblest style of early romanticism, celebrating the imaginative life of the German nation at its most characteristic. And just as Mozart's *Magic Flute* had done, so Weber's *Freischütz* clearly showed that it was in this region that the German musical drama was at home, but that it was locked behind its frontiers. Weber himself experienced this when he tried to lift it over them: his *Euryanthe*, for all its wealth of beautiful detail, must be deemed a failure. Confronted by the task of depicting a conflict of big violent passions in an aristocratic sphere, Weber's strength forsook him; he went about it in a diffident half-hearted way, attempting by means of a scrupulous depiction of individual character-traits to achieve what could only be accomplished by big powerful strokes encompassing the whole; so he lost his spontaneity and became ineffective. It is as though Weber realised that here he had sacrificed his inborn chastity; in his *Oberon* the dying man turned back with a sad smile to the gracious muse of his innocence.

As well as Weber Spohr sought to conquer the German stage. But he could never attain Weber's popularity: his music was too lacking in the dramatic vitality which must issue forth from a scenic representation. All the same, the works of this master are German through and through in the depth and melancholy of their emotional appeal. What is completely missing is the touch of naive gaiety so characteristic of Weber, without which the prevailing tone, especially in dramatic music, becomes monotonous and loses its effect.

As the last and most significant successor to these two, Marschner demands consideration. Since he touched the same chords as Weber he rapidly achieved a certain popularity. But when the works of the new French school took the German nation by storm this composer, for all his inborn strength, was unable to uphold the popular German opera which his predecessors had so brilliantly revived. Indeed the new French dramatic music may be said to have delivered a decisive death-blow to German popular opera; it has virtually ceased to exist. Even so, this more recent period calls for some consideration, since its influence upon Germany has been so powerful, and since it nevertheless seems that in the end the German will dominate this period too.

We cannot do otherwise than date the beginning of this period from Rossini, for it was he who with the splendid carelessness of genius swept away the remains of the old Italian school which had withered into a mere formal skeleton. His gay, sensual melodies winged their way all over the world, and his merits—his facility, freshness and wealth of form—acquired consistency, particularly when they came under the influence of the French. Among them the Rossinian movement acquired character and a national stability which gave it a more dignified aspect. Its French practitioners— maintaining the independence, yet in sympathy with the nation— proceeded to create works of an excellence unrivalled in the history of the art of any one single people. In these works of theirs they expressed the virtue and the character of their nation. Boieldieu's lovely *Jean de Paris* exhales the delightful chivalry of medieval France. The liveliness of the French, their intelligence, their wit, their charm, all flower in that exclusively French genre, the Opéra comique But the supreme achievement of French dramatic music is Auber's insurpassable *La Muette de Portici* (*Masaniello*), a work such as no nation can bring forth more than once. Its power to take by storm, its welter of emotions and passions depicted in glowing colours and saturated with characteristic melodies, gracious yet powerful, charming yet heroic—is not all this a perfect expression of the recent history of the French nation? Could anyone but a Frenchman have created this astonishing work? It cannot be gainsaid: with this work the new French school reached its peak and established its hegemony over the civilised world.

Small wonder then that the receptive and open-minded German welcomed these excellent productions of his neighbour with unfeigned enthusiasm! For when general issues are involved the German knows how to judge more fairly than other people. Moreover these works from abroad met a specific need, for it is undeniable that the genre of dramatic music on a grand scale never took root in Germany—probably for the same reason why the higher type of German play never came to full fruition. On the other hand the German more than any other possesses the power to go to another country, develop its art to its highest peak and raise it to the plane of universal validity. Handel and Gluck abundantly proved this, and in our time another German, Meyerbeer, has provided a fresh example. Now that it has reached a point of complete and absolute perfection the French school has nothing more to hope for than to see itself adopted generally and brought to a similar degree of splendour. But this would be an extremely difficult task. Were a German to undertake it and obtain the glory, he would certainly have to be endowed with that disinterested good faith so characteristic of his countrymen, who have not hesitated to sacrifice their own lyric stage in order to embrace and cultivate a foreign genre that contains more promise for the future and has a more directly universal appeal. Perhaps one day it will come to pass that reason will abolish the barriers of prejudice which separate peoples and that all the inhabitants of the globe will agree to speak one and the same language?

At any rate so far as dramatic music is concerned one can assume that at present the French and the German are identical: when a work receives its first performance in the one country rather than the other the difference is purely topographical. That the two nations are joining hands and reinforcing each other means that the foundations of one of the greatest of artistic epochs are being laid. May this splendid alliance never be dissolved, for one can conceive of no brotherhood of nations likelier to lead to greater and more perfect results for art than between Germans and Frenchmen, since the genius of each supplements what is lacking in the other.

The Virtuoso and the Artist

An ancient legend tells of a priceless jewel whose dazzling sparkle suddenly bestows upon the fortunate mortals who behold it every spiritual gift and all the happiness of a contented mind. But it lies buried deep under the earth. The story goes that in former times certain privileged beings endowed with superhuman eyesight saw it through the chaos of rocks and rubble piled above, like the shattered pillars and broken masonry of a gigantic ruined palace, and that the sight filled them with inexpressible rapture. They were seized by a longing to clear away the debris so that all hearts should be filled with divine love and every mind with blissful knowledge by the sight of that dazzling splendour, beside which the sunshine paled. But all their efforts were in vain: they could not move the heavy mass above the magic stone.

Centuries passed. Through the spirit of those rare privileged beings who had beheld it the jewel's radiant light was still reflected in the world. But nobody was able to get near it himself. Yet it was known to exist and there were tracks leading towards it. So it occurred to men to employ the well-tried techniques of mining to dig it out. Shafts were sunk and mines and galleries built stretching down into the bowels of the earth—a subterranean structure was created, and still they built on, laying down more and ever more tunnels and side-galleries until eventually the labyrinth became so confused that the knowledge of the right way was completely lost. In the end the jewel's very existence was forgotten in all the toil and trouble. The whole crazy structure was abandoned, its shafts, tunnels and galleries left to cave in and collapse . . . until one day, so the story runs, there appeared a humble miner from Salzburg. He carefully inspected the work of his forefathers; the sight of all those countless paths and tunnels leading nowhere filled him with amazement; they seemed to him a portent. Suddenly he experienced a feeling of exquisite joy: through a crevice he caught the sparkle of the jewel. With a single glance he took in the whole vast labyrinth; he could see the way to the jewel, and guided by its sparkling light he penetrated to the deepest depths and found it. For a while a wonderful radiance was shed upon the world filling all hearts with inexpressible rapture. But the miner from Salzburg himself was never seen again.

Another miner appeared, this time from the Siebengebirge near Bonn. He had come in order to find the man from Salzburg lost in the deserted mine. He soon found the trail, and suddenly his eye caught the jewel's magic sparkle and was blinded by the dazzling sight. All his senses seemed to be swimming in a sea of glorious light. Seized by a divine frenzy, he plunged into the giddy depths, and the whole mine collapsed on top of him with a mighty crash as though the end of the world had come. This miner too was never seen again.

So the story, like all miners' folk-tales, ends with a disaster. But here the tale has a sequel. Amid the fresh ruins traces of the old mine were still visible, and in recent times attempts have been made to dig out the two buried miners in the optimistic belief that they might still be alive. At present the work of excavation is being taken very seriously and is attracting considerable attention: people come from far and wide to visit the scene of operations; fragments of rubble are bought as mementoes, since everybody wishes to contribute his mite to the good work; people also purchase stories of the lives of the two lost miners, written with great exactitude by a Bonn professor, except that he was unable to say just how the disaster occurred—only the folk who told the tale know that. Indeed, things have so turned out that the tale itself is being forgotten and that in its place a whole crop of new fables has sprung up. It is said for instance that some of the excavators struck some rich veins of gold and had it minted into solid ducats. And indeed there appears to be something in this: people now seem to be thinking less and less of the magic jewel and of those two miners, although their rescue is still proclaimed to be the object of the enterprise.

Perhaps the whole legend together with the ensuing fable can be understood in an allegorical sense. Its meaning would be easily grasped if the magic jewel were held to represent the *genius of music*. Then the names of the two miners would not be hard to guess. As for the mass of rubbish and rubble that covers them, it lies all around, cluttering the path whenever we attempt to get through to them. Whoever in his dreams has glimpsed that legendary light, whoever in hours of holy rapture has been fired by the genius of music, and then looked round for a means of preserving his vision, stumbles at once over that mass of rubble. He has to get out his shovel and dig; the site is full of gold-diggers churning up the earth and flinging their dross and slag in the way as he attempts to burrow down the old mine. The mass of rubbish grows higher and higher and thicker and thicker; the sweat pours from his brow. Poor fellow! And the people around all laugh at him.

In all this a matter of serious import is involved.

The notes that you write are intended to be sounded: you yourself want to hear them and you want them to be heard by others. It is supremely important, indeed vital, that the notes which are sounded should correspond exactly with your mental image of the composition when you wrote them down. In other words, you demand that your thoughts should be faithfully and conscientiously conveyed to the senses without the slightest distortion. It follows from this that the supreme merit of the executive artist, the virtuoso, is his ability to reproduce perfectly the composer's thoughts, and that this ability is only possessed by the artist who really and truly assimilates his intentions, completely suppressing any invention of his own. No doubt the composer's intentions can only be correctly elucidated in a performance which he himself directs. Next best would be the performer who also possesses a creative gift and who accordingly values fidelity to intention and yet knows how to handle the music with a certain affectionate freedom. With these two one could class the executive artist not endowed with creative power but with the ability to absorb the work of another and treat it as though it were his own. He must have the modesty to suppress his personal characteristics, whatever they may be, so completely that neither his merits nor demerits are noticed. For what matters is that we should hear the work itself, ideally reproduced, and that our attention to it should in no wise be distracted by the special qualities of the performer.

Unfortunately this legitimate demand is completely contradicted by the conditions under which music is performed in public today. All the public's interest and curiosity are directed in the first place to the performer's skill; it is only the pleasure in this which leads to consideration of the work performed. Not that one would dream of blaming the public, that tyrant whose favours we all seek! Nor would it be so bad if it did not have the effect of corrupting the performer by causing him to forget his true function. He is responsible for preserving the dignity and purity of art; for he, the composer's representative, is the medium through which artistic ideas first attain a real existence. His honour as a virtuoso, therefore, is bound up with the honour in which he holds the composer's art; if he treats that art merely as a plaything, then he is throwing away his dignity. Of course, if he has no conception of his dignity, that will not trouble him. But in that case he is not an artist, though he is deploying an artist's skills; these provide no warmth but plenty of glitter, and so the evening passes off pleasantly enough.

Picture the virtuoso holding high revel at his keyboard, running, leaping, gliding, melting, caressing, swooning, and to the right and left of him the public hanging on every finger. Draw nearer to the Witches' Sabbath of such a soirée and try to imagine what you, supposing you were a composer, would have to write in order to suit yourself to such a company. Your first thought would be that just as you, for your part, find the event completely incomprehensible, so the events which take place in your mind when you compose would be completely incomprehensible to the master of the revels over there. Good Heavens! Write music in order to suit *that* man? Impossible! Every attempt would be disastrous. For yours is not a music that dances and pirouettes: it lifts itself into the air and rushes like a hurricane. The company would rock with laughter at your ridiculous antics if it did not first throw you out of the room.

With this sort of virtuoso obviously you can have nothing to do. But probably you went to the wrong concert. For after all there are other virtuosos, some of them fine artists, famous for their performance of great works, to whom indeed, in the chaos of present day music-making, the public owes its knowledge of those works. Here is a placard announcing a recital to be given by such a one, and, yes, thereon the name of Beethoven! That suffices. Here is the hall. We take our seats, and truly it is Beethoven himself who appears amidst those elegant ladies, whole rows of them, and those lively gentlemen with lorgnettes standing in a wide circle behind. Yes, Beethoven is there, sinewy and forceful, with a look of sad omnipotence: he is there, sowing dread in the perfumed heart of all that dreamily swaying elegance. But who is coming with him? Good God!—William Tell, Robert the Devil, and—who next?—Weber, my dear and gentle Weber! I breathe again! But then—O Heavens!—a galop. Whoever has himself written galops, not to mention potpourris, knows the lengths to which one can be driven in order to get near to Beethoven. I understood the dreadful necessity which today still exacts galops and potpourris from one who would proclaim the genius of Beethoven so, while I could not but admire this virtuoso, I cursed his virtuosity. . . . Be warned by it, all you true disciples of Art! Resist the temptation of all that gold lying around as you dig your way down the ruined mine. Keep on digging ever more deeply for the magic jewel. Something tells me that those two buried miners are still alive; if I am wrong, let us at any rate believe they are; what harm is there in believing?

But perhaps this is all mere fantasy? The composer needs the virtuoso and the virtuoso, if he is of the right kind, needs the composer. So at any rate it used to be; in our day something seems to have happened to cause a breach between the two. Certainly in former times it was easier for the composer to be his own virtuoso; but he became over-bold and made things so difficult for himself that he had to delegate the task of performance to people who spend their lives doing the other half of his work for him. Really the composer ought to be grateful. He leaves it to the virtuoso to confront the tyrant public; if he fails, it is he who is hissed, not the composition: should it be held against him that when he succeeds he accepts the applause not on behalf of the composition but as *his* due? Not that that really matters: all you want is to have your piece performed as you imagined it; in other words, that the virtuoso should neither add nor take away but be your very self. Of course that cannot be easy; indeed, obviously it must be very difficult to put yourself completely into another person's shoes. Just you try!

Look for example at the conductor, whose business it is to beat time: of all people surely he is the least concerned with the personal impression he is creating. He is certain—is he not?—that he knows your composition through and through, that he has got under your very skin. It cannot—no, it cannot—be an arrogant desire to assert himself that causes him to mistake your tempo, misread your expression marks, and drive you to despair when you hear him conduct your work? . . . And yet, a conductor too can play the virtuoso. He can employ a whole battery of nuances and inflections in order to persuade the public that it is his doing that the work sounds so delightful. Thus he may think it a nice idea to damp down a loud passage or to take a fast one rather slowly—or to bring in a trombone here or there, or a bit of Turkish music—above all, to help himself out with some drastic cuts if he is not quite sure of a success. Call him a virtuoso of the baton; he is often to be found—mainly in opera houses. One has to take precautions against him, and this one can best do by winning over to one's side the virtuoso proper, that is to say, the virtuoso who does not imitate somebody else but appears as a person in his own right. I refer to the singer.

Since the composer's idea resounds through the singer and issues forth from his mouth as living tone, one might think that here, at least, misunderstanding is impossible. The instrumental virtuoso is playing upon something outside himself, placing his finger now here, now there; he may be misplacing it. But our melody sits within the singer. . . . True, it may not be sitting in quite the right place; he too may be playing, as it were, upon something outside himself. Is there any hope (we anxiously ask) that our melody will touch his heart? Or will we remain stuck in his throat? We were searching for the jewel in the depths; have we merely stumbled upon dross?

One must remind oneself that the singer's voice is also an instrument and that it is a rare one which has cost him dear. And one must remind oneself that the singer's voice—its kind, its quality—is the public's main concern; *how* he sings is less important and *what* he sings is to most people of no importance whatsoever. To the singer himself, however, this last consideration is extremely important: what he sings must be so framed that he can play upon his voice with the minimum effort and maximum effect. Compared to this how slight a violinist's or a pianist's concern for his instrument, a thing built for him to use, which, if damaged, can be repaired. . . . But that precious, temperamental instrument, the voice? Its anatomy is still not fully understood. . . . Write what you like, you composers, but take care that singers enjoy singing it! How shall you learn? By going to concerts, or better still, to salons. But no, you want to write for the theatre, the opera—dramatically. Very well, go to the opera and you will find that you haven't escaped from the concert and salon. Here too you will find a virtuoso with whom you will be compelled to come to terms. And this virtuoso, believe me, you will find the most dangerous of all, since opera is the sphere in which you can most easily be deceived.

Consider the most famous singers in the world, the artists of our great Italian opera who are honoured as beings of a higher order not only in Paris but in every capital city. From whom should you learn but them? Here you discover what the art of song really is. It was from them that the no less famous singers of the great French opera learnt what singing means and learnt that it was not to be taken lightly (unlike the good simple caterwaulers of Germany who imagine that all that matters is that their hearts should be in the right place, namely, just above their stomachs). Here too, you will find composers who understand how to write for real singers, who know that it is upon this that their reputation, their very existence depends, and you can see for yourself how well they do, how honoured and famous they are. But you don't want to compose in that way, you want to owe your success to the quality of your work, not to the vocal acrobatics of a singer? . . . Consider the matter more closely: ask yourself: do these singers lack passion? When they perform their feats of jugglery do they not shudder and tremble? Is there not a deal of difference between (for example) their delivery of the words '*Ah Tremate!*' and a German singer's rendering of the corresponding '*Zittre, feiger Bösewicht!*' Have you forgotten the '*Maladetta!*' which had a distinguished audience wriggling like a crowd of negroes at a Methodist meeting? But perhaps such things do not seem to you quite genuine? You regard them as mere effects at which anyone with any sense would laugh?

All the same they are a form of art, one which these famous singers have carried very far. For though the voice, too, can be treated as though it were a plaything, the play must create an impression of expressing emotion, otherwise there would be no point in raising the voice above the level of normal speech. And emotion of course is what the public demands—emotion such as they do not enjoy when they sit at home over their whist and dominoes. All this, too, may have been different in former times: great masters found great pupils among singers; the marvels which together they evolved live on in tradition, and are often renewed by fresh experience. Certainly it is accepted that singing should have a dramatic effect; our singers are accordingly taught to simulate emotions so thoroughly that you are left wondering whether they will ever recover from them. It is all done by rule; thus after a period of billing and cooing an explosion makes an incomparable effect; none of it has anything to do with real life, but then of course it is precisely that which makes it 'art'.

You still have a scruple: you are worried by the contemptibly insipid music which serves these singers. What called it into being? The will of those same singers, to suit whom it was composed. What in all the world can a true musician have to do with such stuff? . . . What would happen though, if those illustrious demi-gods of the Italian opera were to present a true work of art? Would they catch fire? Would they reflect the sparkle of that magic jewel? Look, there is a poster announcing a performance this very day of Mozart's *Don Giovanni*. Let us go and see for ourselves!

I did in fact recently attend a performance of *Don Giovanni* by the great Italians, and a very strange experience it was: I was thrown into a whirl, for there were some really fine artists, but cheek by jowl with virtuosos of the most ridiculous sort, who scored a much greater triumph. Lablache's Leporello was unsurpassable; Grisi's Donna Anna superb: a beautiful, richly gifted woman, Mozart's Donna Anna to the life; warmth, tenderness, fire, passion, mourning, lamentation, everything was there! She *knew* that the buried miner still lived and her knowledge strengthened my belief. . . . But Don Juan, the cause of all her suffering, was sung by the world-famous baritone,

Tamburini, who throughout the whole of the evening never threw off the fetters this fatal role placed around his ankles. I had already heard this singer in an opera of Bellini and realised why he was so famous: all the Italian 'effects'—the '*Tremate!*' the '*Maladetta*'—were there on parade. But they didn't work: the short fast numbers scurried past like shadows; the recitatives were merely thrown off; everything sounded wooden and lifeless. In short, Tamburini was a fish out of water—and so for that matter the entire public: everybody that evening seemed so curiously well-behaved, so curiously incapable of the usual wild outbursts of enthusiasm. Was this perhaps an act of homage to the genius who was spreading his wings through the house that evening? We shall see. In any case even the divine Grisi was making no great impact; that is to say, her secret passion for the tiresome Don Juan was not properly grasped. . . . And then there was Lablache, that colossus, and yet that evening every inch of him a Leporello. How did he manage it? He chattered and gossiped and guffawed; his knees quivered, he was as fleet as a hare; yet every note of his enormous bass voice was clear and glorious. At one point he emitted a whistle and the sound was as pure as a distant church bell. He did not stand, he did not walk, nor did he dance; yet he was forever on the move, one saw him here, there and everywhere, yet he never obtruded because he was always precisely where his droll presence was needed to enhance the humour or the terror of a situation. And yet that evening Lablache did not get a single round of applause—evidently that kind of dramatic achievement did not appeal to the taste of the public. What really upset the public, though, was that its darling, Madame Persiani (one's heart misses a beat as one writes the very name!) was not heard to advantage in the music of Zerlina. That everybody was preparing to go into raptures over her I had noticed, and having recently heard her in *L'Elisir d'Amore* I could understand why. Decidedly it was Mozart's fault that she was missing the mark tonight—another fish out of water, and such a pretty one! What would Persiani and her public have given for the inclusion of an excerpt from the *Elisir*! . . . As the evening wore on, though, I became increasingly aware that some curious excess of restraint was being exercised on both sides of the curtain: some unspoken agreement seemed to have been entered into which for a long time I was unable to explain. Seeing that the audience was to all appearances in a 'classical' mood, why had that glorious Donna Anna failed to arouse the genuine enthusiasm which one would have supposed to be the whole point of such an evening? Why attend a performance of *Don Giovanni* at all, if one is so loth to be swept away? It really and truly began to look as though some painful act of abnegation had been agreed upon—but for what purpose? Some purpose there must be, for though a Paris audience such as this is free with its money it expects something in return, even though it may be worth very little.

In due course the mystery was solved: *Rubini that evening delivered his famous trill on a top A and top B flat.* That explained everything. So much for all my fine ideas about poor Ottavio, the much ridiculed tenor stop-gap for Don Juan! And really that night I had for a long time felt heartily sorry for the fabulously celebrated Rubini, the prince of tenors. Obviously he found the task of playing this Mozartian role a very thankless one. There he came, the impassive, solidly built man, the divine Donna Anna tugging passionately at his arm—there he came and stood dolefully before the corpse of the prospective father-in-law who now would never bless their union. Rubini, it is said, started life as a tailor and still looks like one—though I myself should have expected a tailor to show a bit more agility: wherever he stood he just stood, making literally no movement at all, for he could sing without moving a muscle; only very rarely did he so much as put his hand to his heart. Nor on this occasion did he appear to have any interest in singing; evidently he was preserving his rather worn voice for some better purpose than to console his beloved with words she had heard a thousand times before. This seemed reasonable enough, and since throughout the whole opera Rubini consistently adhered to this policy I assumed that as far as he was concerned all was over—which set me wondering more than ever what could possibly be the purpose of this singularly ascetic evening. But then something unexpected happened: a general restlessness, a shifting of seating positions, a nodding of heads, a play of fans—in fact all the various signs a cultivated audience gives when suddenly thrown into a state of excited anticipation. Ottavio had been left alone on the stage; as he advanced right up to the prompter's box I thought he was going to make some announcement; but he stood there, and without moving a muscle listened to the orchestral ritornello of his B flat aria. The ritornello seemed to be lasting longer than usual; but this was an illusion: the first ten bars were being inaudibly whispered. When I realised that nevertheless Rubini appeared to be singing I thought that the good man was having his little joke. But the audience looked serious: it knew what was coming. On the F of the eleventh bar Rubini suddenly opened out with such violence that the little passage of triplets leading to the twelfth bar hurtled past like a thunderbolt. Then he instantly resumed his inaudible whispering. I wanted to laugh, but everything became deadly still again. As the orchestra went on with its muted accompaniment and the tenor with his inaudible singing the sweat began to rise on my brow. Something monstrous was being prepared—and really and truly the unheard was followed by the unheard of. The seventeenth bar of the aria was reached: here the singer takes an F which he has to hold through three bars. What can one do with an F? Rubini only begins to become divine on a B flat; he must get *there,* otherwise an evening of Italian opera makes no sense. As a trapeze-artist balances himself on his springboard in preparation for his leap, so Ottavio balanced himself on that sustained F. Through the first two bars he carefully, yet inexorably, increased the volume of his tone. At the third bar he snatched from the violins their trill on the top A and upon the trill itself built up a violent crescendo. At the fourth bar there he sat on the high B flat as though it were nothing at all. Then, executing a brilliant roulade, he plunged before all our eyes back into noiselessness. After that the barriers were down—anything could happen. Every demon was let loose—that is to say, not on the stage at the close of the opera, but among the audience. The mystery was solved: it was in order to witness this feat that the audience had assembled; for this it had endured two hours of abstinence from the accustomed operatic delicacies and tolerated Grisi and Lablache when they took the music seriously. All was redeemed by the bliss of that wonderful moment when Rubini leapt to his top B flat!

I once heard a German poet maintain that despite everything the French are the Greeks of our age, and that there is something Athenian about the Parisians since it is they who have the keenest sense of form. That evening I remembered this remark. That select audience showed not the faintest interest in the content of *Don Giovanni*: in their eyes it was a mere wooden puppet to be wrapped in the drapery of the pure virtuosity which was the formal justification of the work's existence. Rubini alone grasped this; so it was understandable why this cold-blooded elderly gentleman was the darling of Paris, the idol of every cultivated lover of singing. To such lengths had the passion for virtuosity been carried that it alone was the object of aesthetic interest; and the effect of this—the striking effect—had been to deaden the feeling for noble warmth, even the feeling for what was manifestly beautiful. So the noble Grisi, with her beautiful face and moving voice, was unable to touch that audience: presumably she was considered too realistic. On the other hand there you have Rubini: stolid and stout, with well-trimmed whiskers, and elderly to boot—as witness the thickening voice and his care to preserve it: certainly if *he* is set on a pedestal above all others the delight must pertain not to the content, but to the pure aesthetic form. And it is this form which has become obligatory all over Paris: everyone sings *à la* Rubini. The rule is: be inaudible for a while; startle everybody with a sudden explosion; then continue as you had begun, so that you create the effect of a ventriloquist. Already we have Duprez doing exactly this; time and again I look round for another singer hidden somewhere under the stage (like the trumpet representing the voice of the mother in *Robert le Diable*) who suddenly seems to be deputising for Duprez standing near the prompter's box not moving a muscle. That sort of thing is 'art': what can fools like us be expected to know about it? . . . Seriously though, there was some comfort to be drawn from that performance of *Don Giovanni* by the Italians. It proved that great artists are to be found among virtuosos—or, to put it another way, that a virtuoso can be a great artist. Unfortunately the two are closely interwoven, and whoever knows how to distinguish the one from the other feels sad. My heart bled for Lablache and Grisi that evening—whereas I found Rubini uncommonly diverting. Perhaps there is something pernicious about a performance exhibiting such vast differences of quality side by side? The human heart is so fallible, and the road to ruin so very pleasant. Take care not to play with the devil: in the end he comes and takes you unawares. So that evening Tamburini was taken when he least expected it. Rubini had happily swung himself on to his top B flat: from there he could look down upon the devil with a comfortable grin. I thought: God! If only the devil would take *him*!

Frightful thought! The whole audience would have plunged down into Hell after him!

(To be continued in the next world!)

A Pilgrimage to Beethoven

Shortly after the modest funeral of my friend R—, who recently died in Paris, I carried out the wish he expressed that I should write a brief account of his sufferings in the glittering metropolis. Among his literary remains I found the story of his journey to Vienna and visit to Beethoven, told with considerable feeling. Therefore I decided to preface the account of my friend's sad end with these pages from his journal which deal with an earlier period of his life and will serve to awaken the reader's interest in him.

This reminiscence of mine is dedicated to the patron deity of the German musician who has never enjoyed, as I never have, the good fortune of being employed as *Kapellmeister* at a German Court Theatre. I refer to the Goddess of Want and Care. Praise be to thee, thou steadfast companion of my days! Never hast thou forsaken me, never ceased with thy strong hands to ward off good fortune's glaring sunshine and plunge into dark shadow the idle good things of this earth! For thy tireless constancy be thanked! . . . All the same, do please one day seek out another favourite: simply out of curiosity I yearn to know how life might be lived *without* thee. Or, if that is asking too much, confer thy favours upon those political idiots who dream of uniting Germany under a single crown, thereby leaving her with only one Court Theatre. What hope would there be for me then, whose prospects today, when German Court Theatres abound, are dim, to put it mildly? . . . But I ask too much. Pardon my presumption, O Goddess! Diviner of my heart, thou knowest that I have ever been thy faithful servant, and that such I shall continue to be, even were there a thousand Court Theatres in Germany. Amen.

Having offered up this prayer which I offer up every day before I undertake anything I proceed to the story of my pilgrimage to Beethoven.

In the event of this important document being published after my death it is necessary to state who I am, since otherwise much of it would be unintelligible. Give ear, then, whomsoever it may concern!

I was born in a town of medium size in central Germany. What actually I was intended for I no longer remember: I only know that the first time I heard a Beethoven symphony I caught a fever, fell ill, and when I recovered became a musician. Perhaps that explains why, though in the course of time I became acquainted with other beautiful music, it was Beethoven's above all that I loved and worshipped. To steep myself in the depths of his genius became my sole delight; so much so, that I came to imagine that his genius had entered into me, that I formed part of it, a tiny part, on the strength of which I began to build great ideas of myself—in short, to become what most people would call mad. It was a madness, though, which harmed nobody and kept the fool in good spirits, though his bread was very dry and his alcohol very watery (they were earned by giving music lessons, which do not bring in much in those parts).

I had been living in my attic in this way for some time when one day it occurred to me that the man whose creations I revered beyond all others was *still alive*. I couldn't imagine why this thought had never struck me before. Somehow it had never occurred to me that Beethoven was actually there, breathing the air and eating his bread just like anyone else; that he actually lived in Vienna, and that he too was a poor devil of a German musician!

My peace of mind was gone forever. All my thoughts centred around the one wish: *to see Beethoven*. No Mussulman yearned more ardently to visit the shrine of the Prophet than I did to enter the room wherein Beethoven dwelt.

But how was I to realise this wish of mine? Vienna was far away, the journey would cost money, and I had scarcely enough to eke out a bare existence. Since the case obviously called for some exceptional measure, I took along to a publisher certain piano sonatas of mine, modelled on those of the master. The man gave me short shrift: I was a fool, he said, with my sonatas; however, he gave me the advice that if I wanted to make a little money I should try and build myself some slight reputation as a composer of galops and potpourris. . . . I was appalled—but my longing to visit Beethoven triumphed. I proceeded to compose galops and potpourris, albeit with such shame that throughout the whole of that time I could never bring myself so much as to glance at a work of Beethoven.

For this first sacrifice of my innocence I received no money at all, the publisher declaring that before I could expect any I must have first built myself the said reputation. Again I was appalled; but not only that: I grew desperate, and the desperation inspired a series of truly excellent galops, for which I really did receive some money. Eventually I saved enough to carry out my plan. Two years had passed during which I lived in constant fear that Beethoven would die before I made my name as a composer of galops and potpourris. Thank God he was spared to witness that glory—that glory won in order to throw myself at his feet. (Holy Beethoven, forgive me!)

So the great day came when, my purpose achieved, I could tie up my bundle and go. With a sense of awe I quitted the house and turned my steps southwards. I would have gladly travelled by coach, of course—not that I shirked the long walk (what hardships would I not have borne!), but because it would have got me there sooner. My glory as a composer of galops, however, was not such that I could afford the fare. So I bore the hardships, comforting myself with the thought that all the while I was drawing nearer to my goal. Ah, what dreams I had, what raptures! It was as though I were a lover journeying back after long separation to the beloved of his youth!

I reached the lovely country of Bohemia, the land of harp-players and street-singers. In a small town I met some travelling musicians, who formed a small orchestra consisting of a cello, two violins, a clarinet and flute; also there was a harpist and a couple of women singers with nice voices. They played dances, sang songs, received some money and moved on. I met them again on the road at a pretty, shady little place, where they were staying. They were eating lunch; I joined them, explaining that I too was a travelling musician, and we made friends. Since they played dance music, I timidly asked whether they had ever played any of my galops; they answered no, they did not know them. What good that did me!

I asked whether they played anything else besides dance music. 'Indeed we do,' they replied, 'but only among ourselves—not for the gentry.' They brought out some music—and to my astonishment I beheld the great Septet of Beethoven. Did they play that? I gasped.

'Why not?' replied the eldest.'If Joseph here, our second fiddle, hadn't hurt his hand, we should be doing so this very minute.'

Overjoyed, I offered to take Joseph's place as best I could. I seized his violin and we began the Septet.

What a delight it was! Here on a Bohemian country road, under an open sky, a performance of Beethoven's great piece by a band of dance musicians playing with the purity, precision and depth of feeling of the finest virtuoso.

We were playing the Finale when an elegant equipage slowly and noiselessly wended its way up the slope of the road and came to a halt opposite. Within, his legs outstretched, lay an extraordinarily tall, extraordinarily blonde young man attentively listening to our music. Drawing a note-book out of his pocket, he jotted down a few words; then he tossed a gold coin in our direction and ordered his servant to drive on. From his speech we realised that he was an Englishman.

The incident jarred us—it was fortunate that we had reached the end of the Septet. I embraced my friends and offered to attach myself to them—but they were returning to their native village which lay off the main road. I would have accompanied them, had Beethoven not been awaiting me. . . . We took a touching leave and went our different ways. Later it occurred to me that not one of them had picked up the Englishman's coin.

At the very next inn I stopped at whom should I find but the Englishman, enjoying a good meal. He looked at me long and hard. At length he addressed me in passable German.

'Where are your colleagues?' he asked.

'Gone home,' I said.

'Take up your violin and play me some more,' he continued. 'I'll make it worth your while.'

I declared angrily that I did not play for money. In any case I had no violin. In a few words I explained how I had come across the said colleagues.

'They were good musicians,' the Englishman rejoined, 'and that symphony of Beethoven's too was very good.'

This utterance impressed me. Did he make music? I asked.

'Yes,' he answered. 'I play the flute twice a week, on Thursdays the French horn, and on Sundays I compose.'

Did he indeed? I was astonished. Never in my life had I heard of a travelling English musician. To judge from this one with his elegant equipage they must do well. Was music his profession then? I asked.

For some time he did not answer. When at length he spoke the words came slowly. He was, he would have me understand, a man of substance.

It was evident that my question had offended him. Embarrassed, I continued my simple meal in silence.

The Englishman, however, continued to regard me. After a while he addressed me again. 'Do you know Beethoven?' he asked.

I replied that I had never been to Vienna and was on my way there now in order to realise a burning desire to visit the revered master.

'Where have you come from?'—he asked.—'From L—.' 'That's not so far. I've come all the way from England in order to make Beethoven's acquaintance. So we will both of us meet him. He is a very famous composer.'

Of all the extraordinary coincidences! Great master, I thought, to whom some travel on foot, others by comfortable coach, what opposites dost thou attract! . . . Not that I envied my interesting Englishman his proud coach. My toilsome pilgrimage on foot, I felt, was holier and more pious: it could not but lead to a happiness unknown to one who made the journey in pride and luxury.

The post-boy blew his horn and the Englishman drove off, calling out that he would be seeing Beethoven before me.

After a few hours on the road I unexpectedly encountered him again. One of the wheels of his coach was broken; the vehicle had tilted over, and there he was seated inside, majestically calm, and up behind his servant. The post-boy had been sent off to fetch a smith from a village some distance away and they had been waiting for a long time. Since the servant could not speak German, I offered to go to the village myself and rout out the smith and post-boy. I found the latter in an ale-house, taking his ease over a glass of schnapps regardless of his errand; however I soon managed to bring the two of them along to the damaged coach. The wheel was patched up, and the Englishman drove off—calling out this time that he would notify Beethoven of my visit.

Making my way along the road the next day I was extremely surprised to encounter him yet again. This time there was no broken wheel: the coach was drawn up right in the middle of the road, and he was sitting in it calmly reading a book. As I drew near he appeared pleased to see me. 'I've been sitting here waiting for you for hours,' he said. 'It occurred to me that it was very wrong not to invite you to drive with me to Beethoven. Riding is much better than walking. Step into the coach.'

Once more I was astonished. For a moment I was tempted—but then I remembered how, as I had watched him drive away the day before, I had sworn that, no matter what the circumstances, I would make my pilgrimage on foot. I explained this—now it was his turn to be astonished. He had no idea what I meant. He repeated his invitation, pointing out that he had been waiting for several hours, and this though he had been delayed by having to put up at a place where the broken wheel could be thoroughly repaired. I heatedly repeated my refusal and he drove off, bewildered.

By this time I was beginning to feel a certain aversion: a dim premonition was warning me that somehow this Englishman might do me great harm. In any case his reverence for Beethoven and plan to visit him seemed the mere snobbish whim of a rich gentleman rather than the product of a deep inner necessity. I preferred to continue upon my way alone, untainted by such company.

As though Fate intended to prepare me for the dangers of the association, I met the Englishman yet again on the evening of the same day. His coach was drawn up in front of an inn, and since he was sitting in it back-to-front, facing the direction from which I would come, it was evident that he was waiting for me. 'Sir,' he said, as I came within earshot, 'again I have been waiting for you for hours. Will you please step into this coach and drive with me to Beethoven?'

This time I experienced not only astonishment, but dread: the fellow's determination to do me a service seemed only explicable on the assumption that, aware of my growing aversion, he was bent upon my ruin. I accordingly refused him again, still more heatedly. Whereupon he called out, '*Damn it*, you don't seem to think much of Beethoven!—*I* shall soon be seeing him!' and rapidly drove off.

That really was the last time I encountered the son of Albion during that long journey. At length I was walking the streets of Vienna: my pilgrimage had reached its end. With what emotion did I enter that Mecca of my faith! All the hardships of the journey were forgotten, I had attained my goal, I was within the walls which encircled Beethoven.

I was too deeply agitated to attempt to carry out my plan to visit him at once. My first move was to enquire where he lived, so that I could find myself a lodging in the neighbourhood. I chose a rather inferior looking inn just opposite the master's quarters. I rented a tiny room on the fifth floor, and there prepared myself for the greatest event of my life.

After I had stayed there for two days, resting, fasting and praying (I paid no further attention to Vienna itself), I plucked up the courage to cross the street to the queer looking house opposite and climb up the stairs to the master's lodging. Beethoven was not at home, I was informed. That suited me quite well, since it gave me another chance to collect myself. But after I had tried again four times, and each time been given the same information with increasing emphasis, I concluded that this was my unlucky day and gave up.

As I was making my way back to the inn the Englishman greeted me cordially from the first floor.

'Have you seen Beethoven?' he called.

'Not yet; he was not at home,' I replied, amazed by this latest encounter. He met me on the stairs and in the most friendly fashion drew me into his room. 'My dear sir,' he said, 'today I saw you go to Beethoven's house five times. I have been staying in this wretched hotel several days in order to be near Beethoven. Believe me, it is very difficult to make his acquaintance; he is a very moody gentleman. At the beginning I went up to his lodging six times, and each time was shown the door. Now I get up early every morning and sit here by the window until late evening in order to see when Beethoven goes out. But it seems that the gentleman never does.'

'Are you telling me that Beethoven was at home today and refused to see me?' I cried, dismayed.

'He refuses to see the pair of us, that's obvious. And for me very unpleasant, seeing that it was in order to visit Beethoven, not Vienna, that I've come all this way.'

This was very bad news. Nevertheless on the following day I persisted, but never with any success: the door to the shrine remained closed.

Meanwhile my Englishman, who from his post at the window had been following my abortive comings and goings with an anxious eye, made enquiries which established that Beethoven did not dwell on the side of the house facing the street. Although very put out, his determination was unshaken—which was more than could be said for mine: the proceeds from my galops made a protracted stay in Vienna out of the question; nearly a week had passed, and still I had not achieved my purpose. The situation was beginning to look desperate.

I unburdened myself to the innkeeper. He gave me a smile. He would explain the whole cause of the trouble, he said, provided I promised not to betray him to the Englishman. With a sense of foreboding I gave the promise.

'It's like this, you see,' said the honest fellow. 'Lots and lots of Englishmen are always coming here to see Herr Beethoven and get to know him and this annoys him very much—in fact, the constant pestering of these people has thrown him into such a fury that now no stranger has the slightest chance of getting anywhere near him. . . . One has to make allowances; he is a very queer sort of gentleman. . . . Not that it doesn't suit *me*: this inn of mine is usually full of Englishmen staying longer than they intended owing to the difficulty of meeting Herr Beethoven. . . . Now that you've promised to hold your tongue and not drive away all this custom, I'll try and find a way of helping you.'

Pleasant news indeed, all this! Because I, poor devil, was being taken for an Englishman I was being thwarted! Oh my foreboding was all too justified, the Englishman *was* my ruin! . . . My first thought was to move out of the inn, since obviously at Beethoven's place it was assumed that every lodger there was an Englishman on no account to be admitted. However, I was restrained by the inn-keeper's promise to find an opportunity for me to meet the master. Meanwhile the Englishman, whom I now abhorred from the depths of my being, was carrying on every kind of intrigue and bribery, always without result.

At last, after several days had dragged by (during which the pro-ceeds from my galops visibly shrank), the innkeeper advised me to go to a certain Biergarten where Beethoven was to be found at a certain hour nearly every day—and furthermore supplied exact particulars of his bearing and appearance in order that I should not fail to recognise him. I decided to try my luck that very day: since Beethoven always left his house by the back door it was impossible to catch him as he went out; the Biergarten was the only hope. But neither on that day, nor the two following ones, was there any sign of the master. Finally on the fourth day, as once again I was making my way to the fateful Biergarten, I became aware, to my consterna-tion, that the Englishman was stalking me. At his watching post by the window he had observed me going off every day at a certain hour in a certain direction; if I had a clue he was resolved to take advantage of it. All this he explained without the least embarrass-ment. It was his intention to stalk me wherever I went, he declared. In vain I protested that I was merely taking the air for the sake of my health in a common Biergarten, no place for a gentleman like him. His mind was made up, I could only curse my fate. Finally I rounded on him furiously, hoping to get rid of him by a display of rudeness—he merely gave a gentle smile. He was beyond intimidation. To visit Beethoven was his *idée fixe*; nothing else mattered.

And indeed it did actually come to pass that on that very day I first set eye upon the great Beethoven. Impossible to describe my thrill, and at the same time my fury as, seated beside the Englishman, I saw a man approach whose bearing and appearance corresponded exactly with the innkeeper's description. The long blue coat, the ruffled shaggy grey hair—above all, the expression of the face, so like the portrait which had stamped itself upon my memory. Error was indeed impossible: in that first instant I had recognised him! As he strode by with short swift steps I was spellbound with astonishment and reverence.

Observing, as he did, these reactions of mine, the Englishman looked curiously at the new arrival, who chose the furthest corner of the, at that hour, empty Biergarten, ordered a glass of wine and sat back apparently lost in thought. 'It is he!' exclaimed my beating heart. Forgetting my neighbour, I feasted my eyes upon the man whose genius had dominated my thoughts and feelings ever since I had learnt to think and feel. Involuntarily I began to fall into a kind of whispered monologue, ending with the all too significant words: 'Beethoven, is it really thou whom I see?'

Bending over me, my fatal companion caught every word. '*Yes!*' he exclaimed, startling me out of my ecstasy. 'This gentleman is Beethoven! Come along and let us present ourselves at once!'

Enraged and terrified, I held the accursed Englishman back by the arm crying 'What are you thinking of?—Do you want to compromise us?—here in this place?—regardless of all decency?'

'Oh but it's a splendid opportunity,' he replied. 'We shan't easily find a better.' Drawing a kind of music-manuscript book out of his pocket he there and then made straight for the man in the blue overcoat. Beside myself, I grabbed the lunatic by his coat-tails shouting 'Stand back, you devil!'

The fracas had attracted the attention of the stranger. Realising with evident embarrassment that he was the object of the disturbance he hastily drained his glass and rose to go. Whereat the Englishman tore himself from me with such force that one of the coat-tails I was holding came off in my hand. He flung himself in Beethoven's path. The latter tried to avoid him, but the intruder blocked his passage and making an elegant bow according to the latest English fashion addressed him as follows:

'I have the honour to present myself to the very famous composer and very honourable Herr Beethoven.'

Further speech was unnecessary since he had no sooner opened his mouth than Beethoven, after shooting a glance at me, sprang aside and disappeared from the Biergarten with lightning speed. Even so, the inexorable Briton would have gone after him had I not clung furiously to his remaining coat-tail. Eventually he gave up, somewhat surprised, exclaiming in a strange voice '*Damn it*, this gentleman is worthy to be an Englishman! He is a great man and I shall not fail to make his acquaintance.'

I for my part stood there like one turned to stone, paralysed by the turn of events which spelt the end of all my cherished dreams and hopes.

Obviously any further attempt to approach Beethoven in an ordinary way would be completely futile. Since I was almost down to my last thaler it only remained to decide whether to cut my losses and return home or take some last desperate step. The former was too dreadful to contemplate. To reach the very threshold of the sanctuary only to be shut out for ever: how could I bear this and not feel utterly annihilated ? But what last desperate step should I take, what path should I follow ? For a long time I was incapable of deciding. My whole consciousness was paralysed—paralysed by the memory of what I had had to endure when Beethoven shot me that parting glance as I stood there holding the Englishman's coat-tail in my hand. He had taken *me* for an Englishman!

What should I do to exculpate myself? Everything depended upon my finding some way of convincing the master that I was a simple German soul, poor in worldly goods, but rich in enthusiasm for things not of this world.

So I eventually reached the decision to unburden myself in a letter. I outlined the story of my life, explained how I had come to be a musician, how I worshipped him and longed to make his acquaintance, how to that end I had sacrificed two years to the task of making a reputation as a composer of galops, how I had made my pilgrimage and what misfortunes the Englishman had brought upon me, culminating in the cruel situation I now found myself in. The description of my sufferings brought relief—so much so that I began to word the letter with a certain intimacy; I even dared to reproach the master for treating a humble admirer so harshly. By the time I had finished I felt truly inspired; my eyes swam as I wrote the address: 'Herr Ludwig van Beethoven'. Uttering a silent prayer, I then took the letter myself to his house.

As I was returning to the inn, uplifted, whom should I run straight into but—O Heavens above!—the fearful Englishman. From his post at the window he had watched my latest visit and detected my look of joyous hope. He detained me on the stairs in order to question me. 'Prospects are good, then, are they? When shall we be seeing Beethoven?'

'Never again in this life will you see Beethoven!' I shrieked. To which I added: 'Leave me alone, you wretch, we have nothing whatever in common.'

'Indeed we have something in common,' he replied coldly. 'Where is my coat-tail, sir? What right had you to take it away by force? Aren't you aware that Beethoven's behaviour towards me is all your fault? How could he have had anything to do with a gentleman wearing only one coat-tail?'

Exasperated by this throwing of the blame on to me, I cried: 'Sir, you shall have your coat-tail, and may it serve as a shameful reminder of how you offended the great Beethoven and drove a poor musician to his ruin!'

He tried to calm me down with the assurance that he had plenty of coats, every one in excellent condition; all he wanted to know was when Beethoven would be receiving us. . . . I stormed up to my fifth floor, locked myself in and awaited Beethoven's reply.

It is not possible to describe what passed within me when in the course of the next hour I received a small piece of notepaper, upon which the following words were scribbled:

Excuse me, Herr R—, if I ask you to put off your visit till tomorrow morning, since today I am busy with a score which has to be sent off by post. Expecting you tomorrow. Beethoven.

Sinking upon my knees, my eyes blinded with tears, I thanked Heaven for granting me this wonderful boon. Then I sprang to my feet and in a transport of joy danced madly round and round the little room. I can't remember what I danced, but I do recall how horrified I was to find myself whistling the tune of one of my galops. That calmed me down somewhat. I left the room and the inn and, drunk with joy, sallied forth into the streets of Vienna.

The streets of Vienna—my God, in my sufferings I had never given the city a thought! How delightful now its cheerful bustle. I saw everything through rose-tinted spectacles: the typical Viennese superficial sensuality struck me as warm, fresh, vital; the typical frivolous, indiscriminate pleasure-seeking as a healthy, natural receptivity to all things beautiful. I inspected the five daily play-bills. Heavens! On one of them I read: '*Fidelio*, Opera by Beethoven.'

I had to go; never mind the state of my finances. As I entered the auditorium the orchestra was just beginning the overture. They were giving the new revised version of the opera which, under the title of *Leonore*, had already been played in Vienna and accorded the honour of being damned by its discriminating public. I too had never heard the revised version; imagine therefore my delight at the fresh marvels it contained! The Leonore was played by a very young girl—but already in early youth wedded to the spirit of Beethoven. With what ardour, what poetry, what thrilling depth of feeling did she play the extraordinary role. Her name was Wilhelmine Schroeder, and it was her noble achievement that was revealing Beethoven's genius to the German public—on that evening even the superficial Viennese were swept off their feet. As for me, it was as though the heavens had opened; I prostrated myself before the genius who had led me, like Florestan, out of the darkness of tyranny into the light of freedom.

I slept not a wink that night. What I had just been through, and what awaited me on the morrow, were too overwhelming to permit of their being carried over into soothing dreams. In a state of continuous rapture I lay awake, preparing to meet Beethoven. At last the new day arrived; impatiently I awaited the hour when I could pay my morning visit. It too arrived, and I set off, trembling at the thought that I faced the most important experience of my life.

I also faced another hideous ordeal.

Leaning nonchalantly against the street-door of Beethoven's house was the Englishman, my demon! He had bribed the inn-keeper, who had read that note of Beethoven's, scribbled on a piece of open paper, before I had done, and passed its message on.

At the sight of him I broke into a cold sweat. All my transports were forgotten. Once again I was in his clutches.

'Come along and let us present ourselves to Beethoven,' he began.

I tried to help myself out with a lie: I was merely going out for a walk. But he cut the ground from under my feet by explaining with unblushing candour how he had come by my secret. He would leave me only when we had seen Beethoven. I tried to dissuade him amicably—in vain! I flew into a rage—in vain! Relying on my nimble feet I then rushed up the stairs with the speed of an arrow and pulled madly at the door-bell of Beethoven's lodging. Before the door could have been opened the gentleman was beside me, grabbing my coat-tails and saying: 'Don't you try to escape me! I have a right to one of these coat-tails and I won't let go until the two of us are standing before Beethoven.'

Turning on him furiously I attempted to wrest myself free. I was on the verge of committing an assault upon the proud son of Albion— when the door was opened by Beethoven's aged female servant, who, seeing the pair of us in our extraordinary situation, made as though immediately to close it again. Terrified, I shouted out my name, swearing that Beethoven had invited me.

As she stood there giving us doubtful looks—the appearance of the Englishman was obviously suspect—Beethoven himself appeared by chance at the door of his room. I seized the opportunity to step quickly inside in order to make my excuses—but with me went the Englishman holding me fast by the coat-tail—which, however, he did let go, as he had promised, now that the two of us were actually standing before Beethoven. I bowed, and stammered out my name. Although the master could not understand my speech, he appeared to gather that it was I to whom he had written that note. He beckoned me into his room. Taking no notice of Beethoven's look of surprise, the Englishman slipped in beside me.

Here I stood then within the sanctuary—but with my joy ruined by the appalling embarrassment of the Briton's presence. Nor was Beethoven's outward appearance calculated to put me at my ease. His clothes were untidy and informal; he wore a red woollen stomach-band; his long dark-grey hair was dishevelled; his expression gloomy and unfriendly. We sat down at a table covered with paper and pens.

An uncomfortable silence reigned. Evidently it irritated Beethoven to find himself receiving two visitors instead of one.

At last in a hoarse voice he addressed me: 'You come from L—?'

I was about to reply when he interrupted me by picking up a sheet of paper and pencil, which lay to hand. 'Use these,' he said. 'I cannot hear.'

Of course I knew all about Beethoven's deafness and had prepared myself. But it smote my heart to hear that hoarse, broken voice say: 'I cannot hear.' To be poor and joyless, one's only solace one's sovereignty in the realm of sound, and have to say: 'I cannot hear.' In a flash I understood why Beethoven looked as he did: why the deeply care-worn cheek, the sombre angry glance, the tightly drawn defiant mouth. . . .

Confused, hardly knowing what I was doing, I wrote down an apology, together with a brief explanation of the circumstances which had compelled me to appear accompanied by the Englishman. When he had read this Beethoven turned to the latter, sitting opposite dumb and contented, and asked him somewhat angrily what he could do for him.

'I have the honour . . .' began the Englishman.

Beethoven interrupted him hastily. 'I do not understand you. I cannot hear, and neither can I speak very much. Write down what it is you want.'

The Englishman reflected calmly for a moment. Then he drew out of his pocket an elegant looking piece of music manuscript and said to me: 'Good. Write down that I request Herr Beethoven to look over my composition, and if anything should displease him be so kind as to mark the passage with a cross.'

I wrote down every word, thinking that now at last I might get rid of him. And so indeed it proved. After he had read the request Beethoven with a curious smile put the Englishman's composition on the table, gave him a curt nod, and said: 'I will send it to you.' The gentleman appeared perfectly satisfied. He rose to his feet, made one of his most elegant bows, and excused himself.

I gave a mighty sigh of relief. He had actually gone.

Now at last I could feel I was really within the sanctuary. Even the gloom in Beethoven's face began to lift. After looking at me calmly for a moment, he addressed me thus:

'So that Briton has been plaguing you, has he? . . . Then take comfort from me. I've been plagued to death by these Englishmen who come here to stare at a poor composer as though he were some rare wild animal. I'm very sorry I took you for one. . . . You said in your letter that you were satisfied with my compositions. I'm glad to hear it; these days I don't reckon very much on people liking my things.'

As I listened to these simple, intimate words I lost my painful shyness. With a thrill of joy I wrote down that I was very far from being the only one whom his works filled with enthusiasm, and that it was my great longing that he would give my native city, for example, the joy of welcoming him: he would soon be convinced of the enormous impression his works had made on the entire public.

'I can well believe that my works go down better in North Germany,' Beethoven replied. 'The Viennese here are a great disappointment. The trash they listen to every day makes it impossible for them to bring their minds to bear on anything serious.' By way of contradicting him, I told of the performance of *Fidelio* I had attended yesterday, which the Viennese had applauded with the greatest enthusiasm.

'Humph, *Fidelio*,' growled the master. 'There's nothing more to all that hand-clapping than mere vanity, you can take it from me: the people think it was their advice I was following when I made all those revisions. Now they want to repay me for my trouble and so they cry "bravo". . . . They're a good-natured, uncultivated folk; I prefer them to the really clever people. . . . Did you like *Fidelio*?'

I described my impressions of yesterday's performance, remarking that the revisions seemed to me to have gloriously enhanced the total effect.

'A tiresome labour!' Beethoven growled. He continued: 'I am no opera composer—that is to say, there isn't a single theatre in the world for which I'd willingly write another opera. If I were to write one after my own heart people would run away. All that stuff operas are patched together out of nowadays—arias, duets, terzettos and what have you—I'd get rid of and put in its place what no singer would want to sing and no public to hear. Glittering lies, boring sugary trash: that's all they understand. Anyone who composed a true musical drama would be written off as a fool. And so he would be if he tried to get it performed, instead of being content to keep it for himself.'

'And how would you go to work on such a musical drama?' I asked excitedly.

'As Shakespeare did when he wrote his plays!' was the reply, delivered with something like violence. 'Those who make it their business to supply the kind of vocal trumpery, with which any mediocrity can win himself an ovation, would be better employed dress-making in Paris than composing dramas. . . . I'm not made for that kind of sport. I know all the pundits say that I only understand how to write for instruments and that I'll never be at home in vocal music. If by vocal music they mean operatic music, then they're quite right. Heaven forbid that I should ever feel at home there!'

At this point I ventured to ask whether Beethoven really believed that anyone who knew his *Adelaide* would dare to dispute his mastery in the realm of song.

After a short pause the master replied: 'When all is said, *Adelaide* and such things are trifles, which your professional singer takes up because they enable him to display his virtuosity. But why shouldn't vocal music be considered as great and serious as instrumental music? Why shouldn't it receive the same respect from the frivolous singer-folk as a symphony does from an orchestra? The human voice, a far nobler and more beautiful organ than any orchestral instrument, is *there*, a fact of life. Why should it be handled any less independently? What new results might not be achieved? Develop the very thing which sets the voice apart and you throw open fresh possibilities of combination. Instruments represent the primal organs of Creation and Nature; their expression can never be clearly defined and formulated since they convey the primal feelings as they first issued forth from the chaos of the Creation, perhaps even before there was any human heart to hear and feel. The genius of the voice is completely different: this represents the human heart, the separate individual sensibility, limited, but clear and definite. Imagine, now, these two elements brought together and united! Imagine the instruments that convey the primal feelings—those raw wild feelings encompassing the infinite—united with the voice that represents the limited, but clear, definite sensibility of the human heart. That second element, the voice, would have a beneficial effect upon the instruments' expression of the struggle of primal feeling in that it would set it within the framework of a definite, unifying course; on the other hand, the human heart itself, represented by the voice, would be infinitely strengthened and expanded by gathering to itself those primal feelings: for now its former vague awareness of the Highest would be transformed into a God-like consciousness.'

Here Beethoven paused for a few moments as though exhausted. 'Of course there would be grave difficulties to overcome,' he continued with a sigh. 'Voices must have words, and where is poetry to be found worthy of such a union? The poem would be overshadowed: words are too feeble an instrument for such a task. . . . You will soon be hearing a new composition of mine, a symphony with choruses, which will bring home what I've just been saying. Words had to be found, and the task of finding them was a great problem. In the end I decided to use our Schiller's beautiful *Ode to Joy*—a very noble uplifting poem, of course, yet a very long way from expressing what in this case no poem in the world could possibly utter.'

The happiness I felt at receiving out of Beethoven's own mouth these clues to the understanding of his gigantic last symphony, which he had just completed and which nobody knew—this happiness is something which even now I find impossible to picture. I expressed my deep gratitude for the privilege and my delighted surprise at the news of another great composition. My eyes filled with tears—I could have knelt before him.

Beethoven seemed to notice my emotion; with a kind of sad, mocking smile he said: 'You will be able to defend my new work when it comes out. Remember me, when all the pundits think I've gone mad, or at any rate declare that I have. But you, Herr R—, have seen that a madman I am not—though I have good cause to be. People think I ought to write what *they* consider good and beautiful; they forget that a poor devil, deaf as a post, might have his own ideas, and that I can only compose as I feel. . . . If I cannot think and feel their beautiful things,' he added ironically, 'well, that precisely is my misfortune.'

So saying he rose and strode across the room with short swift steps. Deeply moved though I was, I too stood up: I could feel

81

myself trembling in every limb. It was impossible for me to continue the conversation either by gestures or by writing. Moreover I felt that the moment had come when my visit should be brought to an end. Merely to write down a few heartfelt words of thanks and farewell seemed inadequate; better to take my hat, go up to Beethoven and let him read in my eyes what I was feeling.

He seemed to understand. 'You are going?' he asked. 'But you'll be staying on in Vienna yet awhile?'

I wrote down that the sole purpose of my journey had been to make his acquaintance, and that now that I had been granted the great privilege of this interview I intended to start my journey home tomorrow.

'You said in your letter how you earned the money to come here,' he replied with a laugh. 'You should stay on in Vienna and write galops—this is just the place for them.'

I declared that that occupation was a thing of the past: never again would I find an object to make it worth my while.

'Don't be too sure!' he rejoined. 'I'd do a lot better as a composer of galops; as things are, old fool that I am, I shall always be badly off. . . . Have a good journey,' he continued, 'and remember me. Whenever you are in trouble think of me and be comforted.'

I was about to take my leave when he called me back. 'Wait a minute! There's that musical Englishman to be dealt with. Let's see where the crosses have to go!' He picked up the Briton's manuscript and smiling quickly looked it over. Then he carefully gathered up the pages, folded a sheet of paper over them, seized a thick pen and drew over the folder a single colossal cross. 'Here's the fellow's masterpiece!' he said, handing me the package. 'Give it to him from me. . . . He's a donkey—not that I don't envy him his long ears! . . . Good-bye, my dear fellow—think fondly of me.'

Upon my return to the inn I saw the Englishman's servant packing his master's trunk. He too had achieved his goal, and I had to admit that he too had shown a great deal of determination. I hurried up to my room and made my preparations for my return journey tomorrow. At the sight of that cross on the folder containing his composition I laughed aloud—all the same it was a souvenir of

Beethoven, and as such I grudged it the evil genius of my pilgrimage. My decision was quickly taken. I unfolded the sheet, took out my packet of galops and inserted them in place of the Englishman's composition. This latter I then sent to the Englishman, together with a note, in which I reported that Beethoven had declared he had not known where to put a cross and that he envied him.

As I was departing from the inn there was my old fatal companion sitting in his coach. 'My best wishes!' he called. 'You have done me a great service. I am very pleased to have made Herr Beethoven's acquaintance. . . . Would you like to drive with me to Italy?'

'Why are you going there?' I asked.

'I want to make Signor Rossini's acquaintance; he is a very famous composer.'

'Good luck to you!' I called back. 'As for me, to have met Beethoven is enough for one life-time.'

We parted. I threw a last lingering look at Beethoven's house and turned northwards, my heart uplifted and ennobled.

Death in Paris

We have just buried him. The weather was cold and dismal and there were only a few of us. The Englishman was there; he intends to set up a gravestone—it would be better if he were to pay off his debts.

It was a sad business. The sharp air of early winter made it difficult to draw breath. None of us could speak and there was nobody to deliver a funeral address. Nevertheless I would have you know that the man we buried was a good man and a true German musician. He had a tender heart: it made him weep to see how they whipped the poor horses in the streets of Paris. And his disposition was so mild that the street-urchins could elbow him into the gutter and he would make no protest. But unfortunately he also had a tender artistic conscience and, though he had no talent for intrigue, was ambitious. In his youth he had met Beethoven and this had so turned his head that it was never possible for him to find his way in Paris.

It is now well over a year since the day when I saw a magnificent Newfoundland dog bathing in the fountains of the Palais Royal. Dog-lover that I am, I stood there admiring the fine animal until eventually it was called away by an individual who at first attracted my attention simply as the owner of the dog. He was by no means so magnificent: decently dressed, but got up in God knows what provincial style. All the same something about his face arrested me; surely I had seen those features before? . . . Could it be? . . . Was it not? . . . The dog was forgotten and I fell into the arms of my old friend R—.

How delighted we were to see each other again! He was quite overcome by his emotion. I led him to the Café de la Rotonde. I drank tea with rum—he coffee with tears.

Eventually I was able to ask him what in the name of Heaven had brought him from the seclusion of a fifth floor in a German provincial side-street to Paris of all places?

'My friend,' he replied, 'call it an unearthly longing to know what it would be like to live on the sixth floor in a Parisian side-street; or maybe a not so unearthly longing to descend to a second or perhaps even to a first floor one: I'm not yet myself quite clear which it is. The fact of the matter is that I could no longer endure the misery of existence in the German provinces and that without waiting to taste the more elevated misery of a German capital city I decided to fling myself into this world-centre, this focal point into which flows the art of every nation, where people from everywhere find recognition —and where I too hope to realise the modest portion of ambition with which the Almighty—no doubt mistakenly—has charged me.'

'Your ambition is only natural,' I said. 'All the same, that it should have led you of all people here does take me by surprise. Tell me first of all how you intend to maintain yourself during the pursuit of your ambition? How much money are you getting every year? . . . Don't look so alarmed: of course I know you haven't got an independent income; you always were as poor as a churchmouse. But I'm bound to assume that you've either had some luck in a lottery or else have persuaded some wealthy patron or relative to provide you with a sufficient allowance for at least ten years.'

My friend smiled good-humouredly as he recovered from his alarm. 'This is how you worldly-wise fools look at things. I might have known it!' he said. 'Prosaic side-issues of that kind are all you can think of. . . . Dismiss all that from your mind, dearest friend. I am poor—so poor that in a few weeks I literally shan't have a sou. But what of it? I've been told I have talent: would you have me go to, say, Tunis, to make my fortune? No, I've come to Paris! Here I shall find out whether those who said I have talent were deceiving me or whether I really have. If not, the disappointment will be quick, I shall accept it and quietly make my way back home. On the other hand if it turns out that I have, then my talent will be sooner and better rewarded in Paris than anywhere else in the world. . . . Oh, don't smile! Try instead to give me some solid reason that will prove me wrong!'

'Very well, my dear fellow, I won't smile,' I replied. 'Indeed, as I listen to you I'm overcome by a feeling of concern for your future, not to mention that of your lovely dog. You can make do with little, I know; but that splendid beast needs a lot to eat. You intend, I take it, to support the two of you by means of your talent? That is fine—a man's first duty is to support himself and compassion for animals is a very noble thing. Tell me what you are proposing to do with your talent? What are your plans? I want to hear all about them.'

'You do well to ask about my plans,' he rejoined. 'I can give you a whole list; if in nothing else, at least I am rich in plans. First and foremost I have in mind an opera: I have a whole supply of finished and half-finished works as well as any number of sketches of various kinds both for grand and comic opera. . . . Don't raise objections: I know it can't happen overnight and regard it only as the basis of my enterprise; even so, though I can't expect an opera of mine to be performed in the near future, surely I shan't have to wait all that long before hearing whether a director will accept one or not? . . . You are smiling again—but let me go on; I know what you're going to say and I have my answer ready. . . . Of course I know I shall have to contend with difficulties of all kinds; but what will they be due to? Surely only to the competition I shall have to face. Here all the finest talents are assembled, offering their works; directors are bound to subject them to the most careful scrutiny; the mere bungler will never get anywhere: only works of true distinction are accorded the honour of selection. Very well then, I'm prepared to meet that test: I demand no distinction which I do not deserve. Apart from competition what, then, have I to fear? Would you have me believe that here in Paris, too, one must play the courtier—in this capital of a free country where you have a press whose business it is to expose the abuses of officialdom and red-tape and so make it impossible that true merit should be deprived of its accolade from the great incorruptible public?'

'The public?' I interrupted. 'There at least you are right! I entirely agree that your talent would bring you success if it were only a question of the public. But, my dear good friend, you grossly underestimate the difficulty of reaching the public. It is not a competition of talents that you have to face, but of reputations and of personal interests. If you have a reliable and influential patron, well and good; but without that, and with no money in your pocket, the case is hopeless: you'll go under and no one will even notice. There will be no question of esteeming your talent or your work (so much favour is unthinkable): the sole consideration will be your name. Since no reputation attaches to yours, and since it figures in no list of shareholders, you and your talent will pass away unnoticed.'

This speech of mine did not have the desired effect upon my enthusiastic friend. Although put out, he refused to believe a word. I went on to ask whether he had considered ways and means of building himself some small reputation which later on might further the execution of the sweeping plans he had been speaking of?

The question appeared to raise his spirits. 'Listen,' he said. 'You know that instrumental music has always been a great passion of mine. Here in Paris, where there's a veritable cult of Beethoven, surely there's good reason to hope that a fellow-countryman and ardent admirer could easily gain a footing if he were to offer to the public works which, however feebly, attempted to emulate the great man's masterpieces?'

'Allow me a word!' I interrupted. 'That Beethoven is idolised in Paris I don't dispute. What you have to bear in mind, though, is that it is the name, the reputation, that is idolised. Simply in itself the name of Beethoven, attached to a representative work, ensures that its beauties are acknowledged. Attach some other name and no concert manager would take the slightest notice of the master's most brilliant flights.'

'You lie!' broke out my friend. 'Now I know that you are systematically trying to discourage me and frighten me off my path to fame. You won't succeed!'

'Because I understand you I take no offence,' I replied. 'But in any case I must point out that this scheme of yours will encounter the obstacles which face any unknown artist, however important his talent, who attempts to make his way in a place where people are far too busy to look for buried treasure. Both these plans of yours would be a good way of consolidating and further advancing an already established reputation—but neither could itself establish one. Your attempts to get your instrumental works performed will be completely disregarded. Even if they successfully emulate the master's characteristic daring—that daring you so admire—you'll be told that they're bombastic and indigestible and that'll be the end of it.'

'But what if I've already anticipated that objection?' my friend asked. 'What if already I have up my sleeve compositions garnished with those horrible modernistic effects that go down with the superficial public and which even the most important artists haven't disdained in order to ingratiate themselves?'

'Then you'll be told that your pieces are too light and trivial to be played between those of a Beethoven and a Musard,' I replied.

'Oh, my dear chap, now I know where I am!' my friend exclaimed with a burst of laughter. 'Now I know that all along you have been pulling my leg! You always were a queer old bird who liked his little joke!' As he laughed he trod upon one of his lovely dog's splendid paws, causing the latter to give a loud yelp—and thereafter humbly to lick his master's hand as though begging him in future not to treat my objections so hilariously.

'You see how unsafe it can be to take lightly what is meant seriously,' I observed. 'But to get back to the point: what other plans, if any, had you in mind when you exchanged that quiet little side-street of yours for this teeming Paris? Suppose you take my advice and for the time being drop those two plans: what other ways have you considered of establishing yourself?'

'Although it means exposing myself to your curious passion for contradiction I'll tell you,' my friend replied. 'Of one thing I'm certain and that is that nothing is so popular in the Paris salons of today as those pretty and sentimental little songs and ballades which so appeal to the French taste and some of which have even made their way here from our homeland. Think of Schubert's songs and the vogue they enjoy! Now this is a field which suits me to perfection; here I could accomplish something really notable. I'll get my songs performed and then I might have the good fortune that others have had: some modest little composition will be heard by one of the directors of the Opéra and he'll be so carried away by my talent that he'll commission an opera on the spot.'

The dog gave a piercing yelp. This time it was I who had trodden upon his paw in a convulsive burst of laughter. 'Do you really go round with such crazy ideas?' I cried. 'What on earth makes you think? . . .'

'But, my God, don't such cases often occur?' the enthusiast exclaimed. 'Have I got to show you the newspapers in which I've read time and time again how this and that director and this and that famous poet were so carried away by the ballade of some completely unknown composer that they agreed to commission an opera and provide a libretto on the spot!'

'So that's it!' I sighed, overcome by a sudden pity. 'Reading the newspapers has turned your poor honest child-like head! My dear chap, never take any notice of more than a third of the reports you read, and of that third never believe as much as a quarter! Opera directors have other, very different, things to do than listen to ballades and be carried away by them! And anyway, granted that this would be a way of building yourself a reputation, who would you get to sing them?'

'Who else,' he replied, 'than those famous singers who out of a sense of duty and out of the kindness of their hearts so often make a point of introducing the productions of unknown deserving talents—or have the newspapers deceived me in this too?'

'My friend,' I answered, 'Heaven knows I am far from denying that noble hearts beat below the throats of famous singers. Nevertheless—other requirements must be met before they can be expected to bestow their favours. . . . You can easily imagine that here too you face competition, and that only a recommendation of boundless influence is capable of convincing those noble hearts that one is really and truly an unknown deserving talent. My poor dear friend, haven't you any other plans?'

This speech drove my companion into a fury. Beside himself (yet taking care not to tread upon the dog) he turned abruptly away, shouting: 'And if I had as many as there are grains of sand in the sea I won't tell you a single one more! Be off, you are my enemy! . . . But you won't triumph, I'll see to that! . . . Tell me this one thing, though, before we part: how did all those others who managed first to make a name in Paris, and then to become famous, how did *they* begin?'

'Ask one of them,' I replied in a tone of cold irritation. 'Perhaps you'll find out. For my part—I don't know.'

'Come along, come along!' the poor fellow called to his dog as he made to go. Then he turned back to me once more. 'You are no longer my friend and I shall not listen to you!' he cried. 'But remember this: *in one year—yes, in one year—either my address will be known to every street-urchin—or I'll send you a message telling you where to come and see me die! . . .* Farewell!' With a shrill whistle—a dissonance—he summoned his magnificent companion, and the two hurried off with such lightning speed that it was impossible to overtake them.

In the days and weeks that followed, during which all attempts to discover my friend's address proved futile, I came to reproach myself more and more bitterly for having responded as I had done to the poor fellow's artless confidences. Instead of treating them with a—perhaps exaggerated—roughness I should have shown more consideration for the peculiarities of his sensitive, deeply ardent nature. I had meant well: I did my best to frighten him off his course because my knowledge of the man and of his circumstances made me certain that the complex paths his ambition was driving him into would lead nowhere. I should have borne in mind that, although peace-loving and tender-hearted, he was not an easily moved, malleable character; and that his faith in the divine and indisputable truth of art, as he conceived it, had reached such a pitch of fanaticism that he had become hardened and stubborn.

I could picture him now wandering through the streets of Paris convinced that he had only to decide which of his various plans to put into action and—hey presto!—his name would be billed all over Paris. He would give a sou to the first beggar he met, swearing within a few months to make it a Napoléon.

As time passed and my attempts to locate my friend continued to prove futile I found myself—I admit the weakness—gradually becoming infected by his confidence: I anxiously scanned every placard and poster in the hope of finding his name tucked away in the corner of some concert announcement; and (paradoxically enough) the longer the hope remained unfulfilled the more I persuaded myself that perhaps after all he had brought it off, that some important personage had taken him up, that he had received a commission which would earn him honour, glory and Heaven knows what else at a stroke. Why not, after all? Every deeply committed soul is following a star: why shouldn't his star be a lucky one? Why shouldn't a miracle happen and the buried wealth be revealed? The very fact that I never once did see his name as the composer of some overture or ballade merely served to convince me that all the time he was concentrating upon his greatest enterprise; that, scorning all lesser ones, he was engaged in the composition of an opera of at least five acts. True, I never ran into him (nor met anyone who had done) at a publisher's or other such place of musical business; but since I rarely visited those holy places perhaps it was my misfortune (so I thought) not to have penetrated into a region where already his fame shone brightly.

It goes without saying that the change of heart I have been describing did not take place overnight: indeed by the time hope had finally banished doubt and fear it was almost a full year since that day I had encountered him at the Palais Royal with his lovely dog. During that time certain speculations of mine had been so amazingly successful that, like Polycrates, I lived in constant expectation of some imminent misfortune. Since I thought I knew what form the misfortune would take my spirits were low when one day I set out to take my usual stroll in the Champs Élysées.

It was autumn; here and there a leaf was falling and above the Elysian splendour loured a grey sky. I approached the familiar Punch and Judy show. There was Punch still busy at his tricks, maltreating his white cat,[1] and generally defying the forces of law and order until in the end the demonic principle—so strikingly personified by the furious cat—would lay him low with fiendish claws.

As I stood before the little spectacle of Punch's misdeeds I became aware of a voice beside me delivering in German the following extraordinary monologue:

'Splendid, splendid! Where in heaven's name have I been looking all these years when here is the very thing right under my nose? Why

[1] A typical feature of the French Punch and Judy street-shows of the period was Punch's maltreatment of a white cat.

should I despise this stage upon which the most striking political and poetic truths are directly and clearly presented in a form that appeals to the most undiscriminating as well as to the most sensitive public? Punch the law-breaker, who is he but Don Juan? And that cat, that magnificent, terrifying, white cat, is she not the living image of the Commandant on horseback? And how the artistic significance of the drama would be heightened by my music! Imagine them all singing!—especially the cat, yes, the cat! What unsuspected charms I'd call up from that lovely throat! Here she doesn't utter a sound, here she's merely the demon: what a sensation when she pours forth the coloratura passages I shall write especially for her! The glorious portamento of her supernatural chromatic scale! And at that passage bound to become famous: "O Polichinell, thou art lost!" the terrifying sweetness of her smile! . . . What a plan! . . . And Punch laying about him with his stick, what scope there for my percussion! . . . What am I waiting for then? This very minute I'll go to the director! I can go straight to him—here there's no waiting-room—one step and I'm inside the sanctuary—I've only to stand before him and his divinely piercing eye will recognise my genius. . . . Or shall I have to face competition here too? . . . Perhaps the cat? . . . Quick, before it's too late!'

The speaker would have there and then charged into the puppet-theatre had I not recognised my friend and prevented a scandal by holding him back in my embrace.

'Who is it?' he cried. Then, recognising me, he quietly disengaged himself, saying coldly: 'I might have known that you of all people would try to prevent this final step to my salvation. Let me go or I shall be too late.'

Gripping his hands again, I was able to prevent another assault on the puppet-theatre, but I was unable to get him to come away. Meanwhile I had time to examine him more closely. God, how dreadful he looked: I refer not to the shabby worn-out clothes, but to the face! Gone completely was the old open, spirited expression; the eyes were glassy, fixed; and the pale, sunken cheeks, marked with sinister dark-red blotches, spoke not only of worry and trouble, but of—starvation!

My distress as I regarded him appeared to have some effect, for he relaxed his struggle to free himself.

'How are you, dear R—' I stammered. To which I added with an attempt at a smile: 'Where is your beautiful dog?'

'Stolen,' was the curt reply, delivered with a dark look.

'Not sold?' I asked.

'Wretch! Just like the Englishman!' he muttered with a scowl.

I had no idea what he meant. 'Come,' I urged, 'take me along to your lodging, we have a lot to say to each other.'

He began to rave again. 'You'll soon be able to find the way by yourself; the year is not yet up and now I stand on the brink of recognition. . . . What do I care if you don't believe me? What use preaching to the deaf? To believe you have to *see*; very well, you soon shall see—let me go this minute or I'll consider you forever my sworn enemy!'

I tightened my grip on his hands. 'Where do you live?' I insisted. 'Take me there and let us have a good long friendly heart-to-heart talk; even—if you must—about your plans.'

'You shall hear of them when they have been carried out!' he cried. 'Quadrilles! Galops! They are my *forte*! You shall see and hear! . . . Do you see that cat? She'll bring me some good fat *droits d'auteur*! Do you see how sleek she is and how expressively she is licking her lips? Imagine an inspired chromatic *melos* pouring forth from between those rows of pearly teeth, punctuated by cat-like sighs and sobs, the most delicate in all the world! . . . Just think of it, my dear fellow—but no, you can't, you have no imagination!—let me go, let me go, you have no imagination!'

Tightening my grip yet again, I implored him to take me to his lodging. But all his attention was anxiously concentrated upon the cat.

'Everything, everything depends on her!' he raved on. 'Honour, fame, happiness all lie in those white paws. May heaven move her to bestow her favours upon me! She looks friendly—yes, but that's how cats are; friendly, polite, ah so polite! She is however a *cat*, a false and treacherous *cat*! . . . Wait, I've got it!—I'll use force—I've a splendid dog—he'll teach you! . . . Hurrah!—I've won! . . . But—but—*where is my dog?*'

At these last words the madman's voice rose to a shriek. His eyes darted hither and thither seeking out the dog. As his glance fell on the broad avenue a splendidly mounted, elegantly dressed gentleman came riding by, from his face and clothes evidently an Englishman. Beside him, proudly barking, trotted a magnificent Newfoundland dog.

'Ha, I knew it! My evil genius!' my companion burst out furiously. 'My dog! My dog!'

With maniacal strength he wrested himself from me and dashed after the rider, who at that moment had spurred his horse to a gallop, causing the dog to break into a joyous run. Hard though I tried, I could not keep pace with the poor fellow's frenzied pursuit. I could see the three of them disappearing round a side-street leading to the Faubourg du Roule. When I got there they were no longer visible.

Suffice to say that all further efforts to track down my friend proved fruitless.

Moved and agitated almost to a pitch of madness myself, I eventually decided that I would have to abandon the search for the time being. Not that I did not continue to make the most of every opportunity: at every place connected with music, however remotely, I made enquiries. Only in the Opéra did I come upon a subordinate official who remembered a sad, poverty-stricken looking figure who often used to turn up there and sit waiting for an audience. Of the fellow's name and address he naturally had no idea. Even the police could give no information. The guardians of security, it seemed, did not concern themselves with the very poor.

I grew desperate. Then one day about two months after that meeting on the Champs Élysées a letter was forwarded to me by an acquaintance. I opened it with a sense of foreboding and read the simple words:

Dear friend come and see me die.

The address given was in Montmartre; beyond tears, I climbed the hilly way up to one of the meanest looking houses in the narrow side-streets of that quarter. Even so, the house had five stories; evidently that had appealed to my friend. There was nothing for it but to climb up giddily after him. In the event I was rewarded for my pains, for when I enquired after my friend I was directed to a room at the back, where one was denied the worthy residence's front view of a gigantic alley four feet wide, but compensated by an incomparably better one overlooking the whole of Paris.

There I found my poor pitiable enthusiast—in a tiny little room, on a miserable bed, enjoying the superb panorama. His face was far more haggard and his body far more wasted than on that day at the Champs Élysées; on the other hand his expression and manner were far more composed. The dark, wild, maniacal look, the uncanny glow in the eyes, had gone; all signs of expression were faint, almost extinguished. Those dreadful dark red blotches on his cheeks, too, were for the time being gone, as though dissolved in the general decay.

Trembling, but with a calm expression, he stretched out his hand, saying: 'Forgive me, dear fellow, and thank you for coming.'

The wonderfully soft yet sonorous voice in which he spoke those few words moved me even more deeply than his aspect. I pressed his hand, unable to speak for tears.

After a pause in which to collect himself my friend went on: 'It seems to me that it must be well over a year since we met by that glittering Palais Royal. I'm afraid I haven't quite kept my word. With the best will in the world it wasn't possible for me to become famous in one year; on the other hand I'm not really to be blamed for not summoning you punctually to my death-bed at the end of the year: despite all my efforts I hadn't then got quite that far. . . . Oh, my dear friend, don't weep! . . . There was a time when I had to beg you not to laugh!'

I tried to say something, but speech was still impossible. 'Let me speak,' the dying man resumed. 'It is easy for me and I have much to say. Moreover I know that I shan't be alive tomorrow. . . . The tale is a simple one, my dear friend, a very simple one. No singular complications; no startling turns of fortune; no wearisome details. So don't fear that your patience will be exhausted by my fluency just at present—though were things otherwise I might have felt tempted just to ramble on and on, since there have been days, my dear fellow, when I never spoke a single word. . . . Listen! The situation in which you find me makes it unnecessary to tell you that fortune has not been kind to me. Nor need I describe in detail how I came to lose my enthusiastic faith. Suffice to say that it was not upon *rocks* that I foundered—Oh, happy the sailor who goes down in a *storm*! No, it was into a *swamp*, into a *morass*, that I sank. This swamp, dear fellow, surrounds all those proud, glittering temples of art, towards which earnest, zealous fools like me trudge, as though there salvation were to be won. Happy the light-hearted! With a single well-executed *entrechat* they skip over the swamp and there they are. Happy the rich! Their well-trained horses need only the prick of a golden spur and over they go. But woe to the enthusiast who mistakes the swamp for a flowery meadow, falls in and becomes a meal for frogs and toads! . . . Look what they have made of me: not a drop of blood left! . . . Shall I tell you what really happened? . . . Though why should I? You can see for yourself. . . . Enough to say that I am dying not from wounds inflicted on a battlefield, but—how horrible it is to say!—from hunger contracted in waiting-rooms. They are terrible places, those waiting-rooms, and let me tell you that there are many of them in Paris, very many—with plush seats, with wooden benches, heated and unheated, paved and unpaved!

'In those waiting-rooms,' my friend continued, 'I dreamt away a whole year of my life. Many strange things of man and beast, gold and filth, worthy of the Arabian Nights passed through my mind: I dreamt of gods and double-bass players, gleaming snuff-boxes and prima-donnas, satin coats and love-sick lords, chorus-girls and five-franc pieces. Through it all, piercing my heart, throbbing through every nerve, I seemed to hear the wailful ghostly tone of an oboe. Until, after a wilder, more oboe-haunted dream than ever, I suddenly woke one day to find I had gone mad. . . . At least I think that's how it was. I remember it was on that day I forgot to make my usual deep bow to the commissionaire before I left the waiting-room—I never dared go back to that one for fear of the reception I should get. . . . But to return to that day. I staggered out of the room to the entrance of the building and collapsed on the pavement outside. I fell on top of my dog who as usual had been waiting in the street outside for his master to whom it was permitted to wait with other people inside. This beautiful dog of mine, you must understand, had been a great help: it was entirely due to him that the commissionaire had now and again condescended to notice me. But the dog was losing his beauty—hunger was gnawing at his vitals as they were at mine—and this was another worry since it meant that the commissionaire would soon completely lose interest; already I had noticed some contemptuous smiles. . . . As I was saying: I collapsed on top of my dog. How long I lay there on the pavement, unconscious of the kicks I got from passers-by, I have no idea. I was woken eventually by the tenderest of kisses: the warm licking of my dog. I sat up, and in a moment of clarity realised that the most pressing need of all was to find a way of feeding him. A sympathetic *marchand d'habits* gave me a few sous for my worn-out waistcoat. The dog ate away and I contented myself with what he left; this suited him, of course, but while he waxed, I waned. The sale of my grandmother's old ring brought back all his lost beauty: he bloomed —Oh, fatal bloom! . . . The state of my mind grew worse and worse: I no longer remember what went on there—only that one day I was seized by an irresistible desire to pay a visit to the devil. Accompanied by the radiantly beautiful dog I found myself outside the entrance of the Concerts Musard. Perhaps I had expected to find the devil there? That too I can't say. I watched the crowd going in, and whom do you think I saw? That abominable Englishman, the very one, completely unchanged, who, as I once told you, plagued me so during that visit of mine to Beethoven! I was appalled: I had steeled myself to meet a demon of the underworld; it was another matter to have to face this apparition of the upper world. To my dismay I saw that the awful man immediately recognised me. I could not escape him—the crowd was pushing us nearer and nearer. Eventually the Briton was forced to violate the conventions of his countrymen and literally fall into the arms I had raised in order to fight my way out! There he stood, wedged against my poor bosom quivering with a thousand gruesome sensations: it was a frightful moment! However the crowd soon parted sufficiently for him to disengage himself, which he did quite calmly. I would have turned and fled, but that was not yet possible "Welcome, dear sir!" he called. "A pleasure to be always meeting you along my path to Art! Let us go together to Musard." "Go to the devil!" was all I could reply in my fury. "Yes," he said, "I imagine it will be pretty devilish. Last Sunday I drafted a composition which I intend to show Musard. Do you know him? Perhaps you could introduce me?"

'Seized not only by horror but by an indefinable fear, I managed to get out of the crowd and escape along the boulevard with my barking dog behind me. In a twinkling the Englishman was at my side, his hand on my arm: "Excuse me, sir," he asked excitedly, "does that beautiful dog belong to you?" "Yes." "He really is magnificent. I'll tell you what: I'll give you fifty guineas for him. A gentleman needs a fine dog; I've already had a whole number; unfortunately none of them were musical; they couldn't bear it when I played my horn and flute; they all ran away. Since you, sir, have the good fortune to be a musician I take it that this dog of yours must be musical. In which case I can hope that he will also stay with me. Therefore I offer you fifty guineas." "Wretch!" I shouted, "I wouldn't part with him, not for the whole of the British Isles!" Then I rushed off, my dog leaping ahead. We turned down a side-street leading to the place where I usually spent the night. It was bright moonlight; and as I ran I looked back anxiously; to my horror I thought I could see the Englishman's tall figure following me; I doubled my speed; I looked back still more anxiously; now the spectral figure was still there, now it seemed to have vanished. Panting, I reached my refuge, gave the dog his food and lay down, hungry, on my hard bed. I slept long and had terrible dreams. . . . When I awoke my beautiful dog was gone. Whether he had run away or been enticed away through the not properly locked door is something which to this day I don't understand. I called him and searched for him until, gasping for breath, I sank down exhausted.

'You remember how I saw the faithless brute that day on the Champs Élysées and how desperately I tried to recover him? Do you know, he recognised me and shied away from my call like a wild animal? Even so, I kept on chasing him and his satanic master until the man turned his horse through a gate, which closed on the two of them with a bang. I pounded upon it with my fists; the only answer was a furious barking. Worn out, dead to the world, I stayed there leaning against the gate—until I was wakened from my stupor by the sound of a scale being excruciatingly played on a French horn.

It came from the depths of the elegant hotel behind the gate, and was followed by the dull melancholy howling of a dog. Then I let out a loud laugh and went my way.'

Here my friend broke off—not because speech had become difficult, but because the excitement of his tale had fearfully strained him. No longer able to sit up straight, he sank back with a low groan. There was a long pause. I gazed sorrowfully at the poor invalid: that light flush, the unmistakable symptom of consumption, was on his cheeks; his eyes were closed as one asleep; his breath was faint, ethereal. . . .

I anxiously awaited the moment when I could ask in what possible way I could be of service to him. At last he opened his eyes; they shone with a strange dim brilliance as he turned them towards me.

'My poor dear friend,' I began, 'my great longing is to be able to serve you in any possible way. If you have any wish please tell me, I beg you.'

'So impatient for my last will and testament?' he smiled. 'Don't be afraid, you aren't forgotten. . . . But wouldn't you first like to hear exactly why you find your poor brother lying on his death-bed? You see, I would at least like someone to know the whole story and I can think of no one but you who really cares. Don't be afraid I shall overtire myself; I breathe easily; talking is no trouble. . . . In any case there isn't much more to tell. You can imagine that after the point in my story at which I broke off just now outer events no longer had any meaning for me. From then on the story is only of my inner self, for it was then I knew I was soon going to die. That excruciating scale on the French horn which I heard coming from the Englishman's hotel filled me with such an overwhelming disgust of life that I there and then *resolved* to die. Not that I take any credit for the decision, for I have to admit that the choice of whether to live or die was no longer really mine. Something seemed to have snapped inside me, and as the twanging died away I began to feel well and easy in my mind as never before, and then I knew the end was near. Oh, how happy this made me! How I welcomed the dissolution which I could feel creeping through every part of my emaciated body! Impervious to the outside world, I unconsciously went wherever my

99

tottering legs carried me. They brought me up to the top of Montmartre, and I bade the hill of the martyrs welcome and resolved to die upon it. I, too, was dying for a faith and so I could think of myself as a martyr, though nobody had persecuted me—only hunger.

'Here in this room I found a refuge. All I wanted was a bed and to have brought me the scores and papers which I'd left in a miserable corner of the city, never having been able to find a pawnbroker who would take them. So here I lie, resolved to die in the name of God and good music. A friend will close my eyes; my little estate will suffice to pay my debts, and a decent grave will not be lacking. What more could I wish for?'

At last I gave rein to my feelings. 'But why did you wait to summon me only for these last sad rites?' I cried. 'Surely I could have served you before in some way, however slightly! For the sake of my peace of mind tell me this, I entreat you: was it mistrust of my friendship that prevented you from sending for me earlier and telling me how things stood with you?'

'Please don't reproach me,' he pleaded, 'when I tell you I was under a fixed delusion that you were my enemy. By the time I realised my mistake I was no longer responsible for the workings of my mind. I felt I was no longer fit to consort with superior people. . . . Be kinder to me than I was to you and forgive me! Give me your hand and let this debt at least be settled!'

As I gave him my hand I burst into tears. I could see how his strength was ebbing: he could no longer raise himself from the bed; those blotches on his pale cheeks were fading.

'A small piece of business, dear fellow,' he began again. 'Call it my last testament. In the first place I want my debts to be paid. The good people who took me in here and looked after me have made very few demands: they must be paid. Likewise a few other creditors whose names you'll find on that piece of paper. To this end I apply all my property, that is to say, my compositions and this diary here in which I've jotted down various thoughts and ideas about music which have struck my fancy. I leave it to your expertise, my valued friend, to realise as much as possible from their sale and to use the proceeds to pay off my earthly debts. . . . In the second place, I ask you not to beat my dog, should you happen to come across him: his faithlessness, I take it, must have already been fearfully punished by the Englishman's horn: I forgive him. . . . In the third place, I desire that the history of my Paris sufferings be published, with my name suppressed, as a cautionary tale for all such fools as I. . . . In the fourth place, I desire a decent grave without any pomp or decoration; only a few need attend the funeral—you'll find the names and addresses in my diary. May you and they together pay the expenses —Amen!

'And now,' the dying man resumed after a pause compelled by his growing weakness, 'a last word regarding my faith. I believe in God, Mozart and Beethoven, likewise in their disciples and apostles; I believe in the Holy Ghost and in the truth of the one and indivisible Art; I believe this Art to be an emanation of God that dwells in the hearts of all enlightened men; I believe that whoever has steeped himself in its holy joy must dedicate himself to it forever and can never deny it; I believe that all men are blessed through Art and that it is therefore permissible to die of hunger for its sake; I believe that in death I shall attain the highest bliss—that in my life on earth I was a dissonant chord, which death will resolve in glorious purity. . . . I believe in a Day of Judgment upon which all who dared to exploit this chaste and noble Art for the sake of profit, and all who in the baseness of their hearts dishonoured and disgraced it for the sake of sensual pleasure will be fearfully punished; I believe that they will be condemned to listen to their own music for all eternity. On the other hand I believe that the souls of Art's true disciples will be transfigured in a shining heavenly fabric of glorious harmony and be united therein forever—may such a lot be mine! Amen!'

From the radiance in his eye and the extreme stillness of his body I could have believed that my friend's fervent prayer had already been granted. But he still breathed, however lightly and faintly. I could distinguish the words as he whispered very softly: 'Rejoice, O ye faithful, the joy that awaits thee is great!'

Then he fell silent—the light in his eye went out, his mouth sweetly smiled. I closed the eyes and prayed that God might grant me a similar death.

Who knows what was lost forever when that poor humble mortal perished? Was he a Mozart?—a Beethoven? Who knows? Who can contradict me when I assert that in him a true artist was lost, whose works would have enriched the world had he not starved to death? I ask: who can prove the contrary?

None of those who attended his funeral would have ventured to disagree. Besides myself, there were only two; a philologist and a painter. Another had been prevented by a cold; others had been unable to spare the time. As our humble cortège drew near the cemetery we noticed a beautiful dog anxiously sniffing at the litter and coffin. I recognised the animal . . . and looking round saw the Englishman proudly mounted on a horse. Evidently because he was unable to understand why the dog was anxiously following the coffin into the cemetery he dismounted, handed the reins to a servant and joined us.

'Whom are you burying, my dear sir?' he asked me. 'The master of that dog,' was my reply.

He appeared upset. 'It's damned unpleasant for me that that gentleman should have died before I had a chance to pay him for his dog!' he exclaimed. 'I put the money aside and tried to find a way of conveying it to him, although this animal like all the others sets up a howling whenever I play. However I'll make amends by spending the fifty guineas for the dog on a gravestone for the worthy gentleman.' He went back to his horse and remounted it; the dog remained by the graveside. . . . The Briton rode away.

The Artist and the Public

———

When I am on my own and my mind is full of musical noises which at last fuse into a melody revealing to me the essence of my being, so that my heart beats violently and my unseeing eyes shed heavenly tears of rapture, then I often tell myself what an utter fool I am not to be content to stay alone with this marvellous experience, what an utter fool to go rushing out with it to that horrible amorphous mass, the public. As though the right to exercise my talent depended upon its completely meaningless approval! As though that solitary glorious exercise were not worth a hundred times more than its loudest acclaim! . . . Why do artists, in whom the divine fire burns, quit their private sanctuaries and run breathless through the city's filthy streets eagerly looking for bored dull-witted people upon whom to force the offering of an ineffable joy? The exertions, the excitements, the disappointments they endure before they even reach the stage of being able to make the offering! The tricks and stratagems they spend a good part of their lives devising in order to bring to the public something it can never understand! Do they do it because they are afraid that one fine day the historic development of music might come to a standstill? Perhaps precisely today, when all the talk is of stereotyped schools and styles, they feel that to tear up the precious pages of their hearts' histories might snap the bonds which have hitherto magically united kindred spirits across the centuries?

Something strange and incomprehensible seems to be at work; those who feel themselves subject to it cannot but regard its power as fatal. One's first thought is that the case is simply that of the genius's urge to communicate: what rings loud within him must be made to ring out to the whole world! Indeed it is held that the genius is duty bound to give pleasure to mankind—though who imposed the duty God alone knows! Certainly the genius himself is not conscious of it—least of all when his genius is operating. True, he is not expected to be; but when his works are finished and ready, then surely he should feel bound to pay for the enormous advantage he has over his fellow men by giving them the benefit of his creations. But the fact of the matter is that of all people the genius is the least responsive to the call of duty; he can do nothing with it in his art, and neither, I believe, does it govern his dealings with the world. In whatever he does, however foolish, he remains true to his nature as genius, and indeed I believe that his compulsion to find a public is governed rather by some equivocal motive of which he is not fully conscious, yet which is serious enough to expose even the greatest artist to contempt. . . . In any case the compulsion is hard to understand. Bitter experience teaches the genius that it draws him into an inferior world, with which he can only come to terms by adopting an inferior guise. Would not everybody run away if the genius were to expose himself as he really is in his god-like nakedness? Perhaps it is his instinct to do just this; for were he not fortified by a conviction of his utter chastity, how could he, in the act of creation, be consumed by an almost lascivious delight in himself? Yet his first contact with the world obliges him to disguise himself. For there the rule runs: the public must be amused: therefore whatever he has to offer he must bring in the guise of an amusement. It could, I suppose, be said that the genius who forces himself to obey this rule is prompted by a sense of duty, since duty in the nature of the case involves self-denial. But what sense of duty requires that a man should sacrifice his honour or a woman her modesty? On the contrary, duty demands that men and women should be prepared to sacrifice every personal advantage for their sake. But more precious than honour to a man or modesty to a woman is genius to its possessor. For it is his very self. If you injure that self in the slightest particle of its being—a being containing honour and modesty to their highest possible degree—then nothing is left of the genius, absolutely nothing.

It cannot be a sense of duty, then, which drives the genius to accept the terrible self-denial which presenting himself to the public involves. Some secret demonic force must be at work. This privileged being, blessed with unique powers, goes begging. Cap in hand, he seeks the favours of bored, satiated pleasure-lovers, empty-headed snobs, ignorant know-alls, malicious envious corrupt reviewers, and God knows what else that goes to form the public opinion of the day. And the humiliations the poor man has to bear! The martyred saint can smile: his soul is beyond the reach of torture; the wounded warrior dragging his body through the stormy night can smile: his honour and his courage are not smirched; the woman suffering shame and disgrace for the sake of love can smile: her love and her honour are transfigured and shine the more brightly. But the genius who exposes himself to contempt because he has to pretend that he wants to *please*? The world can count itself fortunate that *his* sufferings are comparatively unknown!

No, these sufferings are not undergone out of a sense of duty; whoever thinks so is drawing his idea of duty from a different source: the need to earn one's daily bread, to maintain one's family. These are important motives—but they do not affect the genius. They impel the labourer, the craftsman. They may impel the genius to do the work of a craftsman; but it is not they which drive him to create and then to seek a market for his creations. But precisely this is the subject under discussion, namely, how explain the demonic compulsion which drives the genius to hawk his most precious possession?

Certainly the mysterious interweaving of a multitude of factors is involved: the whole mind of your highly gifted artist—the whole mind, hovering between heaven and hell—would have to be comprehended before the mystery could be solved. No doubt the paramount factor, the one which alone sustains him in his darkest hours, is a god-like impulse to communicate his own inner bliss to the hearts of all men. This impulse is nourished by the genius's belief in himself, which is stronger than any other man's—and which is responsible for the pride that proves to be his undoing when he is dealing with the miserable realities of life. Feeling, as he does, free in himself, he desires to be free in life, to have nothing to do with its necessities, to be borne along light-hearted, without a care in the world. Were his genius recognised he would achieve this, and so he works for recognition. Thereby he creates the impression of being ambitious, but this is not so: what he is striving for is not honour for its own sake,

but for the freedom which is the fruit of honour. Unfortunately all
the time he is mixing with people who are merely ambitious or who
are content to enjoy freedom without honour. How to distinguish
himself from them? In the rough-and-tumble he is constantly being
mistaken for someone that he is not. How uncommonly clever he
needs to be, how carefully he needs to watch every step in order to
keep on the right path and not create a false impression. But clever
in that sense is precisely what the genius is not: faced with all
the meannesses of everyday life the only thing he can do with his
genius is to let it drive him into a perpetual state of self-contradiction:
tricked and fooled at every turn, he finds himself abusing his enormous gifts and letting them run to waste. . . . And yet all he really
desires is freedom to rejoice the world with his works. The desire
seems to him so natural that he cannot understand why it should not
be granted: surely the issue is simply that his genius should be given
the opportunity to manifest itself? He keeps on feeling that surely
he must succeed, if not tomorrow, then the day after. Just as though
there were no such thing as death. And Bach, Mozart, Beethoven,
Weber? . . . Yet surely it must happen some time? . . . What a
misery it all is!

And in the meantime to make oneself appear ridiculous!

When he looks at himself as we are now looking at him, in the
end he too cannot help laughing. And this laughter is perhaps his
greatest danger, since it is just this which gives him the strength
to keep on going back into the mad dance. His laughter, though, is
very different from the mockery of those who laugh at him. Its basis
is pride. He sees himself as he really is, and in the infamous *quid pro
quo* in which he is engaged, this self-recognition is the source of an
overflowing gaiety, of which he alone is capable. So he is saved by
his levity—only to be led thereby into still worse disasters. It is then
that he allows himself to sup with the devil—giving himself the right
because he knows, however many lies he may tell, that his truthfulness will never be sullied; for his sufferings, every nail of them, have
made him feel that truthfulness is his very soul. There is a curious
consolation, too, in the knowledge that nobody believes his lies, that
his deceptions are always seen through. Who would take him for a
funny fellow? . . . Why then does he seek to give the impression

of being one? Because the world leaves him no other way of attaining freedom—freedom, from the point of view of the world, meaning one thing only, namely, money. To have his genius recognised he must make money: that is the object of the whole mad exercise. And so he thinks: 'God, if I were only somebody like Meyerbeer!' Only the other day Berlioz was imagining what he would do if he had five hundred francs to spend. He would not squander it on some ballade not worth five sous, as some unfortunates do; instead, he would engage the finest orchestra in the world and have it perform the 'Eroica' Symphony for him amid the ruins of Troy. . . . One sees to what heights the fantasy of impecunious genius can rise! . . . Not that such things are impossible. Miracles can happen—one happened to Berlioz himself when that wonderful miser, Paganini, honoured him with a substantial present. But that is only the beginning. Such a sign appears to everyone at some time; call it a bribe from hell, for it means that from now on you are an object of envy. 'Why, now you have *more* than you deserve!' The world will cease to offer you even its sympathy!

Lucky the genius upon whom good fortune has never smiled! . . . In any case, genius is such a huge thing, what can good fortune add to it?

So he says to himself, smiling—and then he laughs, his strength renewed, as he hears within a stirring and surging of new sounds, brighter and more glorious than ever. A work such as even he had never foreseen is growing and thriving in the quietness of his solitude. This is it! This will set the world on fire! Off the maniac rushes down the familiar path as though it were all new and fresh and lovely. He splashes into the mud. He collides with a splendidly attired lackey—whom he mistakes for a general and greets respectfully. He bumps into a sack of gold, shouldered by a no less important looking bank official, and gets a bloody nose. These are all good signs! So he goes rushing and stumbling—until at last he finds himself standing once again in the temple of his shame! And everything is back again where it was before, for as the poet has said: '*Alle Schuld rächt sich auf Erden*' (Every fault committed upon this earth avenges itself).

Yet perhaps all this is a blessing in disguise, perhaps some good genius, probably his own, sees to it that his wishes are never fulfilled.

For were he to be made welcome in that curious temple it could only be as the result of a colossal misunderstanding—and what torments of hell could be compared to the agony of the gradual day-by-day clarification of that misunderstanding? It has been taken for granted that you would be reasonable, that you would be prepared to make compromises. You urgently want a *succès*, do you not? Well, here it is guaranteed. You have only to make this and that slight adjustment: there is the singer, there the dancer, there the great virtuoso—go and arrange things with them. There they are standing by that wonderfully curtained doorway through which you have to pass in order to reach the great public. Don't you know that everyone who has trodden that blessed path has had to bring his little sacrifice? How the devil do you suppose that the great Opéra would have survived if it had spent its time bothering about trifles?

Can you tell a lie? . . .

No, I cannot! . . .

Then you will be ruined and treated with contempt, as the atheists are in England. No respectable person will have anything more to do with you! . . .

Nothing for it then but to keep on hoping that your guardian angel will spare you *that* fate—and to keep on being merry and light-hearted—and to keep on patiently toiling. So all may come right in the end.

Best of all—keep on dreaming!

The Opéra Lies Dying

(Report to the Dresden *Abendzeitung*)

Paris, 23 February 1841

Sir,

You have asked me, a poor German musician, to write you reports from Paris, the city of infinite variety, brilliance and filth. For a while I was confused, unable to make up my mind where I should turn in order to comply most effectively with your wishes. I asked myself whether I should move to the neighbourhood of the Tuileries and entertain you from there with accounts of brilliant *coups d'états*, or whether I should transport myself in imagination into the holy sanctum of the Institut and filch some interesting scraps of information about the fine and the applied arts. But the truth is that if I were to attempt to describe these splendours I would be deceiving you: German emigrants in Paris, apart from a few very rare exceptions, are never able to observe the intimate goings-on in the higher circles of Parisian society with their own eyes and deliver convincing judgments about them. I am not suggesting that Germans lack the ability to comport themselves in such circles: I am merely pointing out that these circles represent a world so totally alien to the German way of life that at the very sight of it we become bashful, and lose both the will and the courage to penetrate further. Charming and amiable as these French people are from the outside, one gets the impression that inwardly—towards foreigners at any rate—they are even more reserved than the English, who are gruff both outside and in. In consequence we are usually reduced to cultivating what is commonly called the public domain: we visit official buildings, coffee-houses with their wide array of periodicals and finally—oh, what a relief!—

theatres. Official buildings, coffee-houses and their periodicals I am content to leave to the care of the political newspapers, while *I* turn to the numerous theatres. I should turn just as willingly to the concert halls, if any in the proper sense of the word were to be found in Paris at all.

All the same, how good it is that there is music in the world—and particularly in Paris! Without it, what would we do, all we countless Germans who are not tailors or watchmakers, but musicians! It is a splendid bond, which not only links us to this completely alien world, but also provides us with some degree of appetite for the common life of Paris. So, once more, praise be to music, and also to the happy fact that the Parisians have unanimously decided to adopt music as one of their amusements! Music is the means by which we Germans can come to understand Paris fully, and with its help we can count on grasping its secrets, from the flageolet tones of the singer Duprez down to the genuine flageolets of the balls in the Rue St Honoré. What lies beyond, or what finds expression through other organs you, my brave countrymen, would be well advised to let alone: you would find it all as dark and mysterious as those dismal and incomprehensible pawnbrokers' bills from the Mont de Piété.

For this reason I have decided, when next I have some spare time, to write a history of Parisian music. I shall have a lot to say about the renovation of the Hôtel de Ville, not to mention the fortifications and other matters of growing concern to a musician, because I foresee that before long all such things will be done to the accompaniment of music—as witness the reburial of the victims of the July Revolution and the return of the *cendres de Napoléon*. Incidentally, since the day it was learnt that the national hero had been disinterred still more or less intact, the *cendres* are now referred to, with strict accuracy, as *le corps de l'empereur*, and that delightful Dantan caricature, in which M. Thiers can be seen holding a box containing the ashes of Napoleon under his arm, has suddenly disappeared. Anyway, it is true that there is a project on foot to introduce a huge orchestra into the Chamber of Deputies, where it will be employed to provide recitative accompaniments for speeches like those of Marshal Soult, and, during the intermissions, to impart delicacy and grace to the hubbub raised by the deputies. In Paris *délicatesse* is everything, and music in the Parisian sense provides the most suitable spice for those delicious sauces with which disaster, mourning and all else are dressed. It is clear that my history of music in Paris will take up a lot of my time and, since I have not yet made up my mind whether to write it in prose or in verse, I shall confine my efforts for the time being to bringing you a few superficial titbits from the world of art as it now appears.

To start with, a death notice! The Paris Opéra lies dying. It looks for its salvation to the German messiah, Meyerbeer: if he keeps it waiting much longer, the death agonies will begin. The trouble is this: Auber has grown old before his time, and Halévy has not been making efforts for the past three years. But Meyerbeer, who participates in the local race for fame only at his own distinguished and deliberate pace, has reasons for holding back his newest work, on which all hopes rest. So the Opéra is floundering and has been forced for some time past to seek its salvation in mediocrities. The public, however, is capricious and will bestow its favours only on worthwhile things— a point which, I must admit, has done much to raise it in my estimation. Brilliant reputations and illustrious names may suffice to impress opera directors and impresarios, but the public does not allow itself to be so easily blinded. It is for that reason that only truly outstanding things keep going; and it is for that reason too, that one always sees *Robert le Diable* and *Les Huguenots* turning up again when the mediocrities are forced to withdraw. *Robert le Diable* is particularly not to say uncannily ubiquitous, and if I were Signor Donizetti or Monsieur Rualtz or any of the countless others whose temerity has led to their ruin, I should hate this Robert as if he really were the devil. Meyerbeer's opera has become the most reliable barometer with which to measure the success—or rather lack of it—of these gentlemen's works. If a new opera fails to make an impact, *Robert le Diable* will be brought out again after the first few performances. So that, when one sees its name on the placards again, one knows for certain that the new opera has fallen through. *Robert* is indestructible. In spite of the scandalous performances it often receives; in spite of the fact that even Duprez is now doing his utmost to sing the title role badly and to act it like a mountebank; in spite of the fact that the scenery has become faded and the dancing ragged after 230 perform- ances—in spite of all this, I assure you that *Robert le Diable* is and remains the only opera besides *Les Huguenots* which can bring the public in.

In view of this one can well imagine how greedily M. Léon Pillet, the present director of the Opéra, is awaiting the master's new work, with which he hopes to achieve a great and lasting success. In the meantime the public, and more particularly the director himself, make do with *La Favorita*.

La Favorita, as you no doubt know, is an opera by Donizetti which enjoys a considerable measure of approval. In connection with this opera I have made an interesting discovery which I will now impart to you. It is that Paris lies midway between Germany and Italy. The German composer who writes for Paris feels obliged to abandon a large measure of his pedantic earnestness, whereas the Italian maestro tends involuntarily to become more serious and sedate, to stop playing the fool and to be on his best behaviour. I will desist from drawing conclusions, which would certainly be in Paris's favour, but I will add that *La Favorita* provides immediate proof of the second part of my assertion. Donizetti's music here reveals, beside the recognised merits of the Italian school, those qualities of dignity and good breeding which one misses in all the countless other operas of the indefatigable maestro.

For us Germans, however, this *Favorita* has acquired a fateful patriotic significance. Before it appeared, both public and director were agreed that the Opéra required a new prima donna, and both parties looked with expectant eyes in the direction of Fräulein Löwe. Madame Stoltz, however, who sang this *Favorita,* managed to persuade M. Pillet that, if he wanted the world's best prima donna, he already had this in her own person, and she seems to have argued her case so effectively that he is no longer in the slightest doubt about it. In order to avoid the calamity of possessing the world's best prima donna twice over, he accordingly cancelled Fräulein Löwe's engagement. This is not only a slap in the face for us Germans: it also places Fräulein Löwe in an embarrassing situation. She comes here, turning down the most tempting offers to remain in Berlin, sings with great success at a single public concert and learns the next day, as a result of her success, that the doors of the Opéra are now closed to her until further notice.

Incidentally, this nearly led to another disaster. Maurice Schlesinger, our leading music publisher and Fräulein Löwe's zealous sponsor—a man consequently involved in the dispute on the side of both parties —took offence at some remark that M. Pillet made. Incensed, he reached for his sword and challenged the author of the insult to a duel. M. Schlesinger's seconds, Messrs Halévy and Jules Janin, attempted to settle matters by presenting M. Pillet with a written apology to sign, but he refused to comply, and a time for the duel was fixed. At the eleventh hour, however, the opera director decided to sign the apology, and so averted a calamity which would have struck me too, being as I am tied to both gentlemen by insoluble bonds of industry and ambition. An opera director and a music publisher— what indispensable people for a striving composer!

But, joking aside, it is an upsetting affair, and not least for Fräulein Löwe (whom the newspapers refer to, incidentally, as Loëwe, Looëwe or even Loeuve). On her first appearance in a concert of the *Gazette musicale* she had, as I already said, a triumphant success. She sang *Adelaide* as well as an Italian aria, thus showing us the difference between the German and Italian manner of singing and arousing our curiosity as to what she might do in the French. On all sides it was acknowledged that she would prove a distinct asset here, since besides enormous vocal agility she possesses a beautiful voice, which is unfortunately not the case with the existing prima donnas, Dorus-Gras, Cinti-Damoreau and Persiani.

The concert at which Fräulein Löwe sang was a fairly typical one. The programme consisted almost entirely of works by German composers, among whom my humble self had the honour to figure. One journal did have a few words to say—though they were extremely gentle ones—about the *parfum allemand* of this concert, but on the whole the French appear gradually to be resigning themselves to the fact that when they talk about music they have to utter more German names than French ones. There is still a certain amount of resistance to the idea, and the small private school of Opéra comique composers, a teeming mass of little Thomases, Clapissons, Monpous and so on, are violently gnashing their tiny quadrille-teeth. Not that that will avail them anything: if they do not begin to show signs of growing up, they will soon find themselves chased off their home territory too.

This territory, the Opéra comique, is in a truly parlous state. Dedicated exclusively to the works of the popular French school, it has for some years now been passing through a lamentable period of insipidity, like a river which, starting out lustily, peters out ignominiously in slime and sand. It would take up too much of my space if I were to try to identify and explain the many reasons for the eclipse of this popular institution. It is enough to say that no more striking instance of fading glory can be found than the history of the Opéra comique since that brilliant epoch when Boieldieu, Auber and Hérold formed so intimate an alliance with the character of their countrymen. The best and most imaginative leader of the new French school has, for a number of years, undoubtedly been Halévy. Unfortunately he succumbed far too soon to the temptation of taking things easily, like his predecessor, Auber: that is to say, of writing simply with comfortable nonchalance. He failed to remind himself that he had not come as far as Auber, who really could claim to have created a brand-new form in which he could afford to relax. And so it happened that Halévy, the very talented creator of *La Juive*, produced a considerable row of poor pieces which the public, to its honour, refused to accept. His *Le Drapier* was the last of these operas; from then on he seems to have found his direction again and to have made a serious effort to make a brilliant comeback. This he most certainly succeeded in doing recently with his *Guitarrero*, a piece worthy of the best of periods and the best of masters. This delightful opera has been a decided and undisputed success, and will perhaps be the beginning of a new and brilliant epoch at the Opéra comique. For it is a remarkable fact that successful works of this kind never appear singly, but are followed by others in a similar vein. The reason for this is that the little people whom I have already named need something to emulate in order to shake them out of their idleness and complacency.

Having said a word about the Opéra comique, it is only just that I should add at least half a word about the Théâtre italien. How my heart leaps at the thought of you, thrice fortunate—no, four times fortunate Italians! If I were Louis Philippe, I should say to myself: 'If I were not Louis Philippe, I should like to be Rubini or Lablache!' Speaking on my own behalf, I should certainly rather be one of these than king of France. What a wonderful existence! Demi-gods who never grow old, their whole life is laurels and bank-notes. They rise from a sumptuous dinner and digest it by singing *La Cenerentola* for the three hundredth time before a public swathed in silk and satin, bathed in perfume and enthusiasm; they drive home with charming laurel wreathes instead of ordinary hats on their heads—and retire to bed to dream of their fees. Is that not wonderful? Who could imagine anything better? And, on top of that, everlasting life! Truly, I find it impossible to believe that these people will ever die or even be obliged to leave off singing. 'Rubini, Lablache etc.' seems to have been the refrain for the past hundred years and it will continue like that for at least as many again. Certainly we shall not live to see a change.

All the same, even these demi-gods need to take themselves in hand now and again, for the Paris public has moments of weakness when it suddenly wakes up to the fact that it has now really seen more than enough of *La Cenerentola*. Such fits of melancholy usually lead to the audiences growing thinner: the regular occupants of the boxes, the scented ladies in their velvet gowns, peer vexedly down into the empty stalls, seeking in vain the black frock coats which are so indispensable a background to the proper display of their shimmering toilets. After such ill-tempered evenings our everlasting heroes sometimes feel impelled to put their heads together with the anything but everlasting opera director in order to discuss ways and means of avoiding such upsets in the future. As a result a new opera may be put on or an old one revived. In certain circumstances something sensational might be planned to draw all Parisian eyes to the Odéon. As such we can count the decision of which I have just this moment heard: Fräulein Löwe, to whom, as I have already told you, the doors of the Opéra have been closed, will now make her début with the Italians. And so our fellow countrywoman will not after all have to leave Paris without the satisfaction of a triumph.

To close my report with something really encouraging, let me tell you of the arrival of a great new talent, loudly and unanimously acclaimed by the Parisian public as a musical event of the first order. I am speaking of the violinist Vieuxtemps. This truly outstanding artist arrived in Paris some time ago, preceded by a very substantial reputation. He made his appearance here in the first concert of the

Conservatoire and played a big new concerto of his own composition. Both his concerto and his playing were greeted with great enthusiasm by a very knowledgeable audience, and in my opinion his success, together with his composition, do indeed constitute a musical event of great significance. At last someone has dared boldly to step forth from the endless row of applause-seeking virtuosos with their dreadful *airs variés*, and restore his art to its proper position of dignity! Somebody has dared to stand up in front of the crowd and fill their pampered ears with the sound of a pure and noble piece, chaste in conception, fresh and alive in execution, and to demand for it the exclusive attention of his audience, employing his virtuosity, manifestly for no other purpose than to present it in an ideal light! Such noble intentions deserve recognition, not to say admiration, for themselves alone, but when they are combined with such rich powers of imagination and technique that they actually turn the intention into a resounding success—this cannot be too highly praised. And this remarkable artist, incredible as it may seem, has only just passed his twenty-first birthday! Now, you virtuosos with your fantasias, your variations and your *polacca guerrieras*, bow down low before this stripling and follow his example—otherwise within five years you will all be dead and forgotten!

With this I will close, for I can think of nothing worthier to write about. If I were to go on, I might find myself telling you about the *boeuf gras*, the fatted ox which, according to French seasonal custom, has been dragging its great weight laboriously through the streets of Paris ever since yesterday and will today, so I am reliably informed, dance on the Pont Neuf to a quadrille especially composed by Musard. As you see, even here music comes creeping into my pen. But I assure you, one cannot possibly escape it in Paris, and you should therefore be happy to have chosen a musician to write these reports. For, believe me, only a musician has the power to convey clearly and understandably what Paris is today, at least in the only way that German eyes can hope to see it.

Another report soon, perhaps even without music—

Yours,

Richard Wagner

Farewell Performances

(Report to the Dresden *Abendzeitung*)

Paris, 6 April 1841

There are gloomy days in the life of the Paris public—fateful days
when it is compelled to face the bitter truth that beauty passes and
pleasures change. On such days I feel sorry for the Paris public and
weep a few unseen tears of sympathy. And who would not weep to
experience the misery of such days? These days, or—to be more
exact—these evenings follow on the first days of spring, and they are
both necessary and unavoidable, being rooted in the nature of things
and the immutable laws of existence.

One such day was that on which the Italians gave their last performance of the season, taking leave of Parisian high society with
a rendering of *I Puritani*. No lover painfully torn from the arms of his
beloved, no parting of father from daughter, mother from son has ever
provided a more heartrending scene than the Italian Opera as it tore
itself from the last convulsive embraces of Parisian society. As I
watched, my heart grew soft, and I was moved to address an audacious
question to the fates: why must this thing be? My glance, directed
sorrowfully upwards, lighted on Shakespeare (for he too figures
among the distinguished poets whose portraits are painted on the
ceiling of the Odéon). He looked at me grimly, as if he had just
finished writing *King Lear*, and said: 'Bold Saxon, do you think we
English don't also want to be amused?' I understood, sighed and said
not a word more. But how could I hope to keep my heart from breaking when I was obliged to see and hear what was going on? Everybody was sobbing and cheering and calling on the parting guests for
souvenirs. What could they give? Not locks from their hair, for even

Rubini with his enormous mane would have departed bald-headed if he had tried to satisfy all that eager throng. They got round the difficulty by singing a succession of heavenly arias and duets, with so much expression and fervour that the scenes of mourning grew even wilder. Men plucked out their beards, ladies rent their expensive garments: one half swooned, while the other half threw flowers. I have no idea how it all ended: overcome, I left my box. In the corridors outside I saw attendants and footmen with velvet cloaks and shawls over their arms. Poor souls, they were weeping too!

If this evening resembled the orgy of grief which accompanies the parting of Romeo and Juliet in Bellini's opera, when one is uncertain whether to rejoice in sorrow or mourn in delight, another evening in the Théâtre français left a softer and more sentimental impression. It was the evening on which Mademoiselle Mars gave her definitely final farewell performance. Used as one has become to Mlle Mars's leavetakings, resigned as one had long been to the thought that the celebrated lady might really one day appear for the last time (indeed, many were under the impression that she had already stopped acting some time ago), nevertheless the final decision made an unusually deep impact. The French gathered together that evening in serious and reflective mood to cast a last lingering look on their past. They could not look back on the career of Mlle Mars without recalling the restoration of the monarchy, the empire, the consulate and the revolution. Some indeed went back as far as the Fronde and imagined they had been alive then and had seen Mlle Mars playing comedy. Thus, when the public was taking leave of Mlle Mars, it felt itself to be taking leave of a remarkable past, and when a Frenchman starts thinking of his past, he is liable to become as solid and as solemn as a German. Mlle Mars of course has no rival in exploiting a mood of this sort, and you can imagine the impression she made on this of all evenings. It was weighty, profound, sentimental, melancholy, moving —and resigned.

But Rachel's doings have also been causing some consternation: her 'last appearances' have also been repeatedly advertised. Some people believed that her consumption had advanced so far that she was no longer able to work on the resurrection of Racine. Others saw the situation as it was: a squabble over the terms of her engagement. It concerned the amount of her future pension, a sum of five thousand francs more or less. Rachel gave way—Racine lives again and Victor Hugo will shortly die.

Theatrical affairs of this sort, dealing with engagements and directorships, are usually a subject of great interest and excitement to the vast Parisian public. To a great many people, a change of director has all the significance which others attach to a change of government. And indeed the two things are as a rule closely connected.

The directors of the royal theatres—that is, those which receive a fixed subsidy, such as the Théâtre français, the Académie royale de Musique, the Opéra comique and the Vaudeville—are appointed by the government to run these theatres on their own account in conformity with certain statutes. The posts are good ones and, in conferring them, the ministers see an excellent way of paying for services rendered. The services in question are rendered almost exclusively by the press. A journalist who has supported some particular politician through thick and thin obviously expects some sign of gratitude when that politician is given a ministry. Invited to state what he wants, he usually answers: 'Give me the Opéra'—for everybody takes this to be the most profitable post in the land. Unfortunately there is only one Opéra, but a considerable number of deserving journalists, particularly when ministries change hands so frequently. But there is room for only a single director: how therefore get the previous incumbent out? Money solves the problem. One director may simply be bought out, while for another an entirely new, ideal and unprecedented post is created, such as for instance *inspecteur des théâtres royaux*—and the deserving journalist becomes director of the Opéra. Changes like this occur something like twice a year, as often in fact as a new minister comes to power. The period of office is consequently short, and it can be imagined how busily these people set about ordering their affairs. Most of them are good husbands and fathers and prefer to retire after a year of hasty administration, that is, if they are not appointed ambassadors or even given a ministry themselves. Such cases are not infrequent: it happened only a short while ago that a retired director of the Opéra, M. Veron, was sent to London on an important mission. The horror on the faces of the

Englishmen when they discovered that they were expected to discuss diplomatic affairs with an opera director was said to have been a joy to behold: they were convinced the man would appear in tights with feathers on his head.

The effect of all this on artistic progress can be left to the imagination. Every new director tends to regard the institution entrusted to his care as a machine, a sort of instant printing press for producing banknotes as quickly as possible. The box office is his main concern; after that come the singers, followed closely by the costumes, the ballet dancers (with whom he usually feels most at home) and then, finally, the composers and librettists. These do not on the whole cause the director many headaches: the choice is easy, for there are only three or four who have been given the privilege of writing for the Opéra. He happily accepts what these offer him, gets the costumes and scenery made, then buys shares and tries to keep the existing government in office.

If his composers do not produce enough, or if they deliver stale goods which he fails for all the keenness of his eye to recognise as such, then the director will probably dip into his bag of old scores and put on whatever he happens to draw out. In this way some quite good things occasionally come to light, and it was probably thanks to a wonderfully lucky dip that we were recently regaled with a new production of *Don Giovanni*. This performance of our *Don Giovanni* had a curious effect on me. I wanted to see it again, and I was particularly interested to find out whether this French production would please me more than the recent Italian one, in which I thought those fabulously renowned singers had sung and acted so incredibly badly.

But in fact I do not rightly remember what the singers, dancers and stage technicians of the great Paris Opéra did with our *Don Giovanni*. They sang, acted, danced and produced with so much enthusiasm that eventually in the middle of it all I fell asleep. And in my sleep I dreamed about the two unholy black knights. But to make my dream understandable to you I must first of all tell you the story of the two black knights.

Once, in a little town not far from the city of my birth, I attended a performance given by a travelling theatre company. As the play was about to begin I heard sounds of confusion coming from the stage. Presently a voice, probably that of the manager, emerged from the jumble, crying: 'The hermit! The hermit! Where is the hermit?' As the impatience of the waiting audience grew noisier, the cry took on an urgent, more threatening character: 'Where the devil is that hermit? We can't start without him! Will somebody find that damned hermit?' I heard a voice replying: 'He's still down in the tavern.' An unprintable oath was uttered, followed by a rapid, re-signed command: 'Bring on the black knights!' The curtain went up. From either side a black knight entered. With a grim cry, 'Aha, you'll pay for that!' they rushed at each other and proceeded furiously to fight. At last the hermit arrived, and the black knights went off. But whenever an actor forgot his words or a piece of scenery got stuck, whenever the leading lady was not ready with her change of costume —whenever, in short, the flow of the action was halted, then those unholy black knights would instantly reappear and with their uttered threat, 'Aha, you'll pay for that!' fling themselves furiously at each other.

Since then I have often encountered these black knights again, particularly on artistic occasions, and I must confess that they always fill me with deep horror whenever I see them, sometimes at the most unexpected moments, before my eyes.

In that dream I had in the Paris Opéra when, incredible as it may seem, I fell asleep in the middle of *Don Giovanni*, the two black knights appeared. They fought bitterly and with increasing violence. This time they really seemed to be out for each other's life, and I rejoiced inwardly that I might in this way be rid of the two ogres for ever. But neither wavered, neither gave way. Neither was prepared to die, although their fighting was now so frenzied that the ear-splitting sound of their blows and their blood-curdling shouts woke me. I sat up with a start—to hear the audience cheering. The orchestra had just finished playing the overture to *William Tell*.

So you see what havoc the black knights were wreaking even here! The singer playing Don Giovanni had become hoarse, and the overture and one act of *William Tell* were brought on to save the situation. My dream had exhausted me and I went home.

In the lower house of deputies (by which I mean the Opéra

comique in contrast to the upper house of the Opéra, attended by such notabilities as Mozart, Weber and Spontini)—in the Opéra comique, then, things are now continuing to go merrily. I wrote in my last report about Halévy's *Guitarrero,* and now all that remains for me is to confirm that it is the success I spoke of. This opera has also provided new proof for my views about what sort of composers these members of the modern French school are. All of them have their roots in the Opéra comique: it was there they learned their lightness and sparkle, their predilection for chanson-like melodies and their deftness in the handling of ensembles. Their music is in consequence mainly in the style of witty conversation, combining the refined with the popular. When the French moved into the field of tragic opera, it was a widening of their horizons rather than an abandonment of territory formerly held. They developed, trained and harnessed their strength on their own native soil and then threw themselves on grand drama with the same courage and boldness with which the fairest of their supporters had once mounted the barricades.

What I am here saying can be seen at its most typical in Auber. His home was always the comic opera: it was here he gathered his strength to venture into battle and win a great victory with his *Muette de Portici.* Halévy, on the other hand, is a striking exception. His creative impulse certainly stemmed from grand opera: the force of his personality and of the mixed blood that flows in his veins directed him straight away to the large arena and brought him immediate victory there. Unfortunately it happened too soon: he seemed to be a man without a past, and it was in order to make this good that he subsequently returned to the cradle of French music. In comic opera, however, he had difficulty in finding the right note. In order to appear light and elegant, he deemed it necessary to become vapid and superficial. He became facile on principle and unfortunately carried this facility back into his old territory. One is repelled by the struggle between frivolity and seriousness in his *Guido et Ginevra.*

But in recent times Halévy seems to have discovered how to catch up on the traditional schooling he had missed. He has concentrated his forces more and more on the comic opera, and his *Guitarrero* is both a proof of good intentions and a sign that he now feels at home there. Who knows whether he is not, like Auber before him, at this very moment preparing his main assault from the ranks of the Opéra comique ? It is certainly being said that his newly completed opera *Le Chevalier de Malte,* written especially for the Académie, contains excellent things.

Auber, too, to whom opera composing has become as much a habit as soaping is to a barber, is again putting in an appearance at the Opéra comique. But the great maestro now often restricts himself merely to soaping, sometimes even only to working up the preliminary lather; it is seldom that one feels his fine sharp blade, clean as it still is. When he does apply it, it can happen that he has overlooked a notch or two in it, and then he unintentionally pulls one's hairs abominably. In this way the customers sometimes leave the barber's shop with their beards still long and can do nothing else but wipe the lather off, unless they prefer to wait until—highly perfumed as it is—it evaporates of its own accord, which happens as a rule even before they have reached home.

All the same *Les Diamants de la Couronne* (the title of Auber's newest opera) is by no means negligible. Now and again the black knights appeared to frighten me, but their fight was never very earnest or embittered, and usually the right man appeared in time. One was always aware that the opera had been written by a master hand: professional expertise can never be missed.

The librettos of the new comic operas are usually Portuguese. Scribe passionately loves the land of Donna Maria. And indeed Portugal is remarkably convenient: it lies a good long way from Paris and no omnibus goes there, so the author has no need to fear that anyone will ever see through his geographical humbug. In Portugal Scribe can do what he wants and everyone is delighted, for it is obvious that he knows the country well, what with all his accounts of events and descriptions of places of which nobody else has even heard. Who could be expected to know those underground caves— and in Portugal of all places!—where counterfeiters lurk and where young unmarried queens lose their way looking for someone to manufacture false crown diamonds, which would enable them to pawn, or even sell the genuine ones whenever they get into financial difficulty ? Here we must indeed bow to Scribe and place ourselves confidently under his guidance, or we should go in constant fear of bruising ourselves terribly at every corner.

You see therefore how important it is for a librettist to take careful stock of outlandish localities in foreign countries and to look in particular for hidden tunnels: it was by doing this that Scribe succeeded in stumbling on that rich vein of gold which is at present filling his coffers. Long live Portugal!

Subjects dealing with the time of Louis XV, Madame Pompadour and Madame Dubarry, which for a while so dominated the stage and particularly the wardrobes of the Opéra comique, are now going completely out of fashion. In a reflective moment it occurred to Scribe to ask what he was getting from these expensive mistresses with their crinolines and their powdered hair. Extravagant as they are by nature, he eventually found himself having to pay their debts if he wanted to avoid a revolution. Of course, he still had the beautiful satin dresses and the golden tresses, but satin quickly wears out and false tresses grow rusty and black—and who would give him a penny for them then? Scribe understandably felt the need for something more dependable, and—since there is little of that nature to be found in Paris—what better choice could he have made than Portuguese queens, particularly when—as in *Guitarrero*—he could get powerful bankers to support them?

Bankers! They are worth a chapter in themselves. And, since they have now come up, I cannot avoid paying them in passing a little respectful attention.

So let me tell you that Liszt recently gave a concert here. He appeared alone: nobody else played or sang. The tickets cost twenty francs each, and he earned a total of ten thousand francs, with no expenses. He is soon to give another concert. What assurance! What infallibility! I am speaking of course of the speculative aspect; his playing is so assured and so infallible that it is not worth wasting a single word on that. The black knights appeared—or rather the overture to *William Tell* by Schiller, arranged for the piano by Rossini and played by Liszt; and it was followed by many other wonderful things. Unfortunately I have no understanding for matters of this kind and can therefore give you only a layman's opinion. Indeed you can spare me even that, for you heard the wonder-man in Dresden yourselves not so very long ago. So I need not tell you who he is and what he does—much to my relief, for truly I should not know how to set about it. On this particular day I developed such a violent headache, such agonising twitchings of the nerves that I had to go home early and lay myself to bed.

Living just opposite me is Henri Vieuxtemps. He saw me return-ing home ill and, friendly soul that he is, he came over, bringing his violin. He sat down beside my bed and played me something, free of charge. I fell into a pleasant slumber and heard in my dreams some lyrical outpourings by Goethe. I wandered through his fields and meadows, I drank at his springs and breathed his fragrant air. My eyes gazed up into the clear ether and there, in broad daylight, I saw in the middle of the sky a divine star which penetrated my being like the blessed eye of Mozart himself. My spirits revived. When I woke, Vieuxtemps was still standing beside me with his violin, calm and relaxed as if he had just performed a good deed. I thanked him, and we spoke no more about it.

Eternal dreamer that I am! From talking of bankers I have invol-untarily come back to musicians. Well, that is the way I am. I have no talent for speculation and nothing good will ever come of me. I am worst of all as a correspondent, and I pity you for having to put up with me. To atone for my 'reprehensible tendency to dream' I should, I suppose, now write a calm and detailed report on Vieux-temps. But, having let out the secret of our friendship and betrayed my gratitude for his happy act of healing, I stand in danger of being accused of praising Vieuxtemps for purely partisan reasons, or be-cause he gave me a home cure for headaches. Yet, however calmly I write, I cannot help praising him right up to the skies. But if Ole Bull were to read this, he might also want to be praised to the skies and, now that I have given away my secret, I should be exposed to the risk of his coming one day to my bed to play his *Polacca guerriera*. One must try to avoid such irritations, and so I will hold my peace about Vieuxtemps, who anyway stands in no need of my help: hundreds of French pens have now made it impossible for anyone to say anything new or significant about him. He has come upon us like a thunderbolt and created his own new epoch—an epoch of such lasting worth that it will raise standards in all branches of art. He has now gone to

England and will soon be passing like a demi-god through all parts of the earth, slaying black knights.

Already his influence has made itself clearly felt, as indeed it should, in the concerts of the Conservatoire, that citadel of true and genuine music. It was here that Vieuxtemps's first appearance was rapturously received, and here it was that the next man to follow him learned exactly what he needed to do if he wanted to preserve his reputation. This man was the violinist Heinrich Ernst, who is an excellent player in his way. At the Conservatoire there were no complaints about his virtuosity, but the same audience that had just heard Vieuxtemps's concerto could not refrain from showing its displeasure with Ernst's concertino, thereby giving this otherwise popular virtuoso a much needed lesson.

Artists who appear at the Conservatoire concerts would in any case do well to look to their laurels. We Germans sometimes tend to take a far too superficial view of the veneration in which these concerts are held. Their audiences really do consist of music-lovers and connoisseurs of the keenest and most fastidious kind. Though they may have started out with only a mediocre preparatory training, constant exposure to masterly performances of great works has necessarily brought them to a high standard of appreciation. The orchestra —and particularly the strings—could not be bettered. We Germans may pride ourselves on having the truest and most intimate *understanding* of the works of Mozart and Beethoven, but the best *performances* of them are given by the French—or at least by the orchestra of the Conservatoire. Listen here to Beethoven's last symphony and you will have to admit that there are parts of it which you are really understanding properly for the first time. I well remember how certain passages in the first movement of this work came as a revelation to me—and they were the same passages which, in performances heard in Germany, had always seemed to me unclear or unimportant. Here they affected me so profoundly that they shed a new light on what the great master was trying to convey.

However, should there still be things in Beethoven's compositions which have escaped the Conservatoire orchestra, all doubts should soon be finally resolved, for Schindler is here—Beethoven's man, the intimate friend, Schindler in person. He has left his home, driven by his master's voice to go out and preach to the heathens; for the light has not yet dawned in the world, we are still groping in the dark, ignorant of the master's mighty teachings. I must speak in priestlike tones, for the man to whom I refer is an anointed man—indeed he bears a striking resemblance to one of the apostles, whose appearance I cannot at the moment recall. He has a bold air about him, his manners are mild and his eyes lively, and he goes about with a brown coat over his shoulders and usually a portrait of Beethoven under his arm.

Schindler has chosen to begin his missionary work in Paris, and one can be quite sure that he has done so in order to demonstrate his courage and steadfastness by venturing straight away among the most dreadful heathens of all. And in truth he will have a hard time of it, for the godless Parisians do not believe a word he says and, even worse, treat him as a figure of fun. He would get on better perhaps if he were able to laugh; but since he cannot bring himself to laugh at the most ridiculous thing of all, which is himself, I fear Paris will prove his undoing. Maybe his character will harden in time and he will come to the conclusion that the world is not worthy of being enlightened by him. But that would certainly be a pity, the more so when one recalls the docile and conciliatory qualities he recently demonstrated. He had seen fit in his book about Beethoven to pronounce a sentence of excommunication on a brochure published in Paris in order to help raise funds for the proposed Beethoven memorial: the brochure was written by Anders and it contains a French translation of the famous biographical notes on the great composer written by Ries and Wegeler. Anders, who was a pupil of the eminent music historian Johann Forkel and is himself one of the most painstaking and knowledgeable of musical bibliographers, was incensed when the normally benevolent Schindler impertinently accused him of the most heinous sin a conscientious writer can commit—the sin of deliberately distorting those notes of Ries and Wegeler through additions and inventions of his own, and shamelessly presenting Beethoven to the French as a sort of wild man of the woods. When Beethoven's disciple arrived in Paris he was gracious enough to offer Anders an interview, in which he undertook to demonstrate the truth of his assertions. The interview took place. The weather was dull that day and Schindler's mood remarkably conciliatory. After Anders had proved to him line by line that he had not made the slightest addition of any significance to the original notes, the lively eyes of Beethoven's disciple filled with tears and, in an excess of docility, he seized Anders's hand. *If he had known him*, he declared, he would never have taken such a liberty, and he solemnly promised in the second edition of his book to make a *handsome apology*.

I have used this example to show how humble the great Schindler really is and how mighty the strength of his astounding logic. It grieves me therefore to see him wasting his eminent gifts of expatiation on the godless Parisians. May his guardian angel soon lead him away from here!

I see, my dear sir, that I have again chatted on without mentioning many important matters which cry out for consideration. Once again, therefore, I must refer you to my next contribution and until then crave your indulgence.

Richard Wagner

Berlioz and Liszt

(Report to the Dresden *Abendzeitung*)

5 May 1841

I see that I shall have to take the bull by the horns if I am to speak
about Berlioz, for the subject refuses to come up of its own accord.
The very fact that, when I write reports on the daily doings of the
Parisian world of entertainment or art (call it what you will), I can
find no occasion to mention this man of genius seems to me revealing
enough. And it also provides me with a good way of introducing my
remarks on Berlioz, who has every reason to claim the right to figure
prominently in my reports from Paris.

Berlioz is no incidental composer, and therefore I could not
expect to light on him incidentally. He is in no way related to and
has nothing whatever to do with the pompous and exclusive art in-
stitutions of Paris: the Opéra as well as the Conservatoire hurried
anxiously to close their doors at the very first sight of him. Berlioz
was forced to become and to remain an absolute exception to long-
established rules, and such he is and always will be, both inwardly
and outwardly. If you want to hear Berlioz's music you will have to
go where he is, for you will encounter him nowhere else, not even in
the place where Mozart appears side by side with Musard. You will
hear Berlioz's compositions only at the concerts which he himself
gives once or twice a year. These are his own exclusive territory, and
here he has his works performed by an orchestra of his own making
before a public captured by him in the course of a ten-year campaign.
But nowhere else will you hear anything by Berlioz, except perhaps
in the streets or in the cathedral, where he is summoned from time
to time to take part in some politico-musical state occasion.

Berlioz's isolation is, however, not confined only to these external circumstances. The main reason for it lies within himself: however French he is in his character and ideas, however deep his sympathies with his fellow countrymen, he nevertheless stands alone. There is nobody to whom he can look for support, nobody beside him on whom he can lean. From our Germany the spirit of Beethoven has wafted across to him, and there have certainly been times when Berlioz would have dearly liked to be a German. At such moments his genius urges him to write as the great master wrote, to express the things he sees expressed in the master's works. But the instant he takes up his pen the natural ebullience of his French blood begins to assert itself—that same blood which raced through Auber's veins when he wrote the explosive last act of *Masaniello*. But Auber was lucky—he did not know Beethoven's symphonies!

Berlioz knew them, however—more, he understood them. They had thrilled and inspired him, yet he was constantly reminded of the French blood in his veins. He sensed that he could not be like Beethoven, but he also felt that he could not write like Auber. And so he became Berlioz and wrote his *Fantastic Symphony*, a work at which Beethoven would have laughed, just as Auber laughs at it, but which was able to raise Paganini to the height of ecstasy and win its composer a following which has ears for no other work but this. Hearing the *Fantastic Symphony* played here in Paris by Berlioz's own orchestra, one has the feeling of being confronted with an unparalleled wonder. A huge inner richness, an imagination of heroic strength hurls out passions like an erupting volcano: colossal clouds of smoke seem to belch forth, lit by flashes of lightning and streaks of flame, causing them to part and change their shape. Everything is huge, bold, but infinitely desolating. Beauty of form is nowhere to be seen and nowhere a quiet and majestically flowing current to whose steady movement we could gladly abandon ourselves. After the *Fantastic Symphony* the first movement of Beethoven's Fifth would have come on me like a blessing.

As I have said, Berlioz's music is inherently French: were this not so, or were it possible for him to change his nature, one might have been able to regard him as a worthy pupil of Beethoven. But his French characteristics prevent him from ever making direct contact with the genius of Beethoven. The tendency of the French is directed outwards in a search for common points of contact in extremes. A German prefers to withdraw from social life in order to seek the sources of his inspiration inside himself, whereas the Frenchman looks for inspiration to the remotest reaches of society. The Frenchman, whose first thought is to entertain, seeks to perfect his art by raising the tone and level of his intercourse, but he never loses sight of the main object, which is to please as large an audience as possible. In consequence the all-important factor is and remains for him the outward effect, the immediate impact. If he has no inner imagination, he will be content with this outward effect alone. If he is endowed with genuine powers of creation, he will still make use of effect, though only as his primary and most important means of getting his message through to the public. What inner conflicts must therefore arise in an artist's soul such as Berlioz's when on the one hand his lively imagination urges him to explore the profoundest and most mysterious depths of his inner being, while on the other hand the demands and peculiarities of the people to whom he belongs, and whose sympathies he shares, oblige him to express his thoughts only on the immediate surface—when indeed his own creative impulses compel him in this direction? He feels that the language of Auber is far too puny for the strange and indefinable things he has it in him to say, yet he also feels that he must use this language, or something like it, if he is to catch the ear of the public. And thus it is that he falls into that confused and bombastic manner of expressing himself which attracts and stupefies the gaping crowd, while those who might well have been capable of understanding his intentions are so repelled that they cannot bring themselves to make the effort.

Another drawback is that Berlioz appears to enjoy his position of isolation and strives obstinately to maintain it. He has no friend whose advice he would respect, no friend whom he would even permit to point out the occasional flaws in his work.

I especially regretted this when I listened to his *Romeo and Juliet* Symphony. In this work there are so many examples of tastelessness and so many artistic blemishes, ranged side by side with passages of pure genius, that I could not help wishing that Berlioz had shown it before the performance to a man like Cherubini, who would certainly have known how to remove a large number of its ugly distortions without in any way harming the original as a whole. Berlioz is so hyper-sensitive, however, that not even his closest friend would dare to make such a suggestion. On the other hand he makes such an astonishing impression on his audience that he is held to be a unique phenomenon incapable of being measured by any known standards, and for this reason he will always remain imperfect and perhaps shine out only as a remarkable, but passing exception.

And this would be a great pity. Were Berlioz to take to heart the many excellent things that the recent brilliant period of modern French music has produced; were he to swallow his pride, abandon his isolated position and base himself on the music of some worthy present or past epoch, he would inevitably exert such a powerful influence on France's musical future that his memory would be assured for all time. For Berlioz is not only a composer of originality and talent: he also possesses a virtue which is as unusual among his fellow composers in France as the sin of coquetry is to us Germans. His virtue is that he does not write for money, and anybody who knows Paris and the ways of French composers will appreciate the value of this virtue in this country. Berlioz is a sworn enemy of everything vulgar, beggarly or catchpennyish. He has vowed to strangle the first organ-grinder who dares to play any of his tunes. Terrible though that vow may be, I have not the least fear for the life of any such street virtuoso, for I am convinced that no one is likely to treat Berlioz's music with greater contempt than a member of this widespread musical fraternity. All the same, it cannot be denied that Berlioz is well able to write a truly popular composition, though here I use the word 'popular' in its most ideal sense. When I heard his symphony written to commemorate the reburial of the victims of the July Revolution (*Symphonie Funèbre et Triomphale*) I had the vivid feeling that every street-urchin in blue shirt and red cap must have understood it down to the very last note. Of course I should feel inclined to call it a national rather than a popular understanding, for it is quite a long step from *Le Postillon de Longjumeau* to this July Symphony. But truly I feel tempted to give this work of Berlioz's precedence over all the others. It is big and noble from beginning to end: what it may contain of morbid exaltation is checked and overridden by a patriotic enthusiasm raising the lament to the lofty peak of its final apotheosis. When I furthermore place to Berlioz's credit the noble treatment of the military band instruments, which were all he had at his disposal, then I must take back—at least as far as this symphony is concerned—what I previously said about the likely fate of Berlioz's compositions: I gladly predict that this July Symphony will continue to live and provide inspiration as long as a nation that calls itself France exists.

I see that I have now done my duty by Berlioz handsomely enough, particularly in regard to length and breadth, and so I feel it is only right and in line with my obligations as your correspondent to pass on now to topical matters.

In the very first of these I find myself back with Berlioz again, for I wish to say something about the concert given by Liszt, with Berlioz conducting, to raise funds for a Beethoven memorial. A wonderful treat! Liszt, Berlioz and in the middle, at the head or at the end (wherever you will) Beethoven! One might ask the Almighty, the creator of all things—but ask Him what? Better not question, but rather admire the wisdom and beneficence of a providence that brought forth a Beethoven! Liszt and Berlioz are friends and brothers, both of them know and revere Beethoven, both draw vigour from the miraculous fountain of his wealth, and both know that they could perform no better deed than to give a concert for Beethoven's memorial. But there is a difference between them; Liszt earns money without expenses, whereas Berlioz has expenses but earns nothing. After putting his financial affairs in order with two very profitable concerts, Liszt thought this time only of his *gloire*: he played for needy mathematical geniuses and for the memorial to Beethoven. How willingly would we all give concerts for Beethoven! But Liszt can actually do it, and at the same time supply proof of the paradox that it is wonderful to be a famous man. Yet how many things would and could Liszt do if he were not a famous man—or rather if people had not made him famous! He would and could be a free artist, a little god, instead of being what he now is—the slave of a tasteless, virtuoso-worshipping public. All this particular public demands from him is miracles and meretricious rubbish. He gives it what it wants, basks in its favour and plays—in a concert for

Beethoven's memorial—a fantasy on *Robert le Diable*! It was done, however, with some reluctance. The programme consisted exclusively of Beethoven's works, but that did not prevent a raving audience from calling thunderously for that fantasy, Liszt's most popular showpiece. It was a point in favour of this very talented man that he threw out a few angry words—'*Je suis le serviteur du public; cela va sans dire!*'—before sitting down at the piano and rattling the favourite piece contemptuously off. So is one punished for one's sins. One day Liszt will be called upon in heaven to play his fantasy on the devil before the assembled company of angels—though perhaps that will be for the very last time!

Among Berlioz's many admirable qualities one must mention his ability as a conductor: he demonstrated this once more at the concert under discussion. There are strong rumours that he is to be made chief conductor of the Opéra, while Habeneck, the present conductor, will take over Cherubini's position as director of the Conservatoire. The only obstacle in the way is Cherubini's life. Everyone is waiting for him to die, probably so that one can start giving concerts for his memorial, since he has already in his lifetime been so wickedly forgotten.

It is really incredible that the composer of *The Water Carrier* lives here in Paris, yet in not one of the thousand places at which music is made is it possible to hear a single note of *The Water Carrier*! I am devoted to all things new and stand second to none in my support of fashion, being of the firm conviction that its dominance is as necessary as it is powerful. But when fashion goes to the length of consigning a man like Cherubini to total oblivion, then I feel like returning to the old dress suit in which I was confirmed and which I wore when I heard *The Water Carrier* for the first time.

All the same, old operas are revived now and again. I look back with real delight to Isouard's *Joconde*, which was played at the Opéra comique last winter: my heart was full, though the house was very empty. I remember asking myself that evening why M. Clapisson writes operas at all, when there is really no need for them as long as one still has *Joconde*. But the needs of men—and particularly of opera directors—are very strange. They often commission plays and operas which they know in advance are worthless, which will fail, which nobody wants to hear and for which they are nevertheless prepared to pay twenty thousand francs. God knows what they want them for! Such was more or less the case recently with an opera by M. Thomas, *Le Comte de Carmagnola*. It had only two acts, was ridiculously boring, failed resoundingly—and yet the director of the Opéra had paid the above-mentioned sum for it—probably as compensation for the *droits d'auteur*, which of course bring in very little for a failure. As you see, one can make one's fortune here!

It has just occurred to me that I have not yet said anything to you about Kathinka Heinefetter, and this delightful and pretty young singer is more deserving than most of a prominent place in a German correspondent's report. Having, as you know, made her début in *La Juive*, she continues to win for herself a firm place in the public's favour. She can pride herself on having achieved a veritable triumph at that first appearance: not only did the opera director withdraw his support from her on that occasion, but he actually went to the lengths of employing the powerful claque *against* his débutante. Certain strange complications had persuaded the director that this action was necessary. What saved Frl. Heinefetter was, first and foremost, her own fine talent, but also the fact that the director made his intentions only too apparent. Everybody took her side, and it was delicious to see the 'Lions' in their boxes mocking the *chevaliers du lustre* (by which name the members of that illustrious organisation, the claque, are known) by clapping her furiously. Frl. Heinefetter's position is now secure, and her talents, combined with the hard work and modesty with which she applies them, enable one to predict confidently that the Opéra has found in her one of its brightest ornaments.

Things have gone less well for Frl. Löwe. I have already told you of her first success and the outcome of this success in relation to an engagement at the Opéra. I also told you that she had been engaged by the Italian Opera. I can now confirm this, though I must add that the engagement extends only to the London season, so that this German singer has still made no stage appearance in Paris. She is consequently restricted to singing in concerts, and I am sorry to have to report that her subsequent appearances have not repeated the success of her first *Gazette musicale* concert. Her choice of songs has certainly been very unfortunate. If one made allowances the first time for her choice of *Adelaide*, a composition which is not really suited to her talents, one did begin to feel surprise when she continued to sing this song practically to the exclusion of everything else. It was in vain that she sought to relieve the monotony of her public appearances with arias by Graun and his like. On the contrary, Graun's wretched aria did much to precipitate her downfall. The French found these interminable old-fashioned roulades too foolish for words, and I must confess, good Christian though I am, that I found myself reduced to laughter by them. So what could one expect from the Parisians, who do not believe in anything—not even in Graun? It is possible—and much to be desired—that Frl. Löwe will repair her somewhat damaged reputation through her appearances with the Italian Opera in London. But even there she will find victory no simple matter, for one must admit, taking things by and large, that Grisi is also worth a thing or two and will not easily be put in the shade.

However, let us not concern ourselves with what might or might not happen in London; I must remain in Paris, and unfortunately there will soon be nothing of importance to occupy my pen. Summer is coming, and with it *coups d'état* and revolutions—matters from which a German musician is obliged to hold his distance. All the same, I shall provide my report with a brilliant, political historical ending: what could be more historical, more political and more brilliant than the baptism of the Comte de Paris and the accompanying display of fireworks? Even more (not to forget my music!), what could be more scintillating than the *concert monstre* which is going to take place in a few days' time in the Louvre gallery? Louis Philippe will be there, and I have been told in strict confidence that, to the strains of an aria by Auber, he will renounce the throne. That will provide an exciting scene and, since I am now urgently in need of rest, I must be careful *not* to accept a pressing invitation to attend this concert (with the idea that I should write a suitably laudatory piece about it for the *Abendzeitung*). I shall therefore leave it to your political correspondent to report on the concert and confine myself to the christening and the fireworks.

The venerable Notre Dame received the young count (who, as

you know, is three years old) with friendly respect and listened in astonishment to the speech which (as I am told by somebody who was standing close by) the young man delivered from the font. In the evening this same Notre Dame appeared in a blaze of Roman candles, rockets and squibs. It had been set up for convenience's sake not far from the Tuileries and was constructed entirely of wood, paper and gunpowder. Every stone, every pillar, every ornament of the grand mother-edifice had been copied down to the smallest detail. Everybody raved and cheered: I myself had the feeling that I could see the hunchback up above. The crowd pushed and shoved. I was grateful to the government for taking the precaution of staging a special fireworks display at the Barrière du Trône for the wicked Faubourg Saint-Antoine, in order to keep the naughty inhabitants of that suburb at a safe distance.

You see, I am becoming political. I had therefore better stop here, for further sorties into the realms of baptisms and fireworks are bound in the end to lead me into byways from which I might perhaps only be rescued by the next concert in the Louvre. But since this coming *concert monstre* with its five hundred musicians is also beyond my strength, the only way I can avoid disaster is hastily and respectfully to sign myself off as

Your obedient servant,
Richard Wagner

Der Freischütz

Oh, my dear German fatherland, how can I help adoring you, even if only because it was your soil that produced *Der Freischütz*! Must my heart not go out to a people that loves *Der Freischütz*? That still believes in fairy tales? That still, having reached man's estate, responds with sweet shudders to the mysteries before which it trembled when its heart was young? Delightful dreamers, with your devotion to forests and evening hours, to moon and stars and clocks in village steeples striking seven! Happy the man who understands you, who can share your raptures, who can believe and feel and dream with you! How happy I am to be a German!

These were the thoughts, along with many others defying expression, which recently pierced my heart like a voluptuous dagger. I felt a searing pain, which shot up into my head. Yet it was not blood that flowed, but tears—the most delicious tears. What the occasion was that drove this blissful dagger through my heart I can reveal to nobody in this huge fine city of Paris; here almost everybody is French, and the French are gay and witty people, full of jokes. Their gaiety would certainly increase, their quips and jokes fall even faster, were I to try and tell them what it was that gave me that divinely beneficent wound.

But you, my gifted fellow-countrymen, you will not laugh. You will understand when I tell you that it happened at a passage in *Der Freischütz*—that passage in the first act when the peasant lads seize their girls by the hand and dance with them into the inn, leaving the young hunter bridegroom seated alone at a table outside. There he was, brooding over his misfortunes, while the evening grew darker and the sounds of the dance music faded into the distance. As I watched and listened, my tears began to fall, and my neighbours in the Paris Opéra thought some terrible misfortune had befallen me. As I dried my eyes and polished my glasses, I resolved to write about *Der Freischütz*. This performance by the French provided me with a mass of material for my projected essay. But, in order to deal with it, you must allow me to do what the French themselves so inordinately enjoy doing—to follow the processes of logic and therefore begin from the beginning.

As you doubtless appreciate, my fortunate countrymen, there is no people on earth so perfect that it cannot profit now and again by taking a look at what the people of another country has to offer. You know it and can speak from rich experience. So it happened that the most perfect nation in the world—for that, as the whole world knows, is what the French consider themselves to be—one day decided to follow the general example and examine what its worthy neighbour could provide in exchange for the thousand and one splendid things it had itself so amiably lavished year by year on other nations. They had heard that *Der Freischütz* was supposed to be very fine, so they resolved to give it a closer look. They had not forgotten a play with charming music which had already been performed before them some three hundred times and which was said to have been based on this very *Freischütz*. This piece, entitled *Robin des Bois*, had, they were assured, been made as logical and enjoyable as it was possible for French hands to make it. But this understandably left them with the feeling that all the good things in *Robin des Bois*—particularly because it *was* so enjoyable—were due to the French; that what they had seen and heard had been, virtually, a French piece interlaced with a few nicely-turned couplets of foreign origin, and they had consequently still to see the genuine German article. They were, of course, quite right. And so it came about that the director of the Opéra, in his capacity as keeper of the French artistic conscience, decided to put on *Der Freischütz* exactly as it is—obviously with the purpose of demonstrating to the Germans that Parisians, too, know what it is to be fair.

I ought, however, to mention that there is another version of this Parisian *Freischütz* saga. It is said that the poetic stimulus was provided by a speculative music publisher, and that the prudent opera director lent a willing ear because his box-office returns were at a very low ebb, owing to those artistic bankruptcies to which even the solidest of French banker-composers seem to have become eternally prone. There was much to be said, therefore, for taking the desperate step of raising a loan from so accredited a bank as the German house of Freischütz.

Whatever the cause, there was no lack of fine phrases to fit the occasion. There was talk of an act of homage towards a thoroughly deserving foreign masterpiece. And, since we are in the habit of taking the French implicitly at their word when they assure us of the unselfish nature of their enthusiasms, we should not dream of suggesting that anything different was meant here. In any case, the decision was made: *Der Freischütz* would be given exactly as it is. The principal reason for that may indeed have been that the version known as *Robin des Bois* was the property of the Opéra comique, and consequently could not be used in the Opéra. But, on the other hand, this adaptation had proved by its extraordinary success that something splendid lay behind this *Freischütz* worth going to the trouble of discovering: namely, gold and silver and banknotes. And so the opera director set up a committee of investigation, consisting of all the great men of his empire, to help him in the task of unearthing the treasure.

The committee met, but all it could discover in the first place were the tremendous difficulties facing it in trying to make this uncouth foreign marksman presentable in such august surroundings as their great opera house.

There was one huge obstacle at the very start: the text was not only illogical, but it was also in German, which nobody—and least of all a Frenchman—could understand. However, there was a way round that: an Italian was chosen to translate the illogical German textbook into French. A happy thought indeed, but in the important matter of what the piece was to be called, neither the Italians nor the French could provide an answer. *Il franco arciero* sounded much too Italian, and *Franc-tireur*, though a German might understand it, would be incomprehensible to a Frenchman. So it was decided to do what an information bureau does and simply call it *Le Freischutz*, which at least nobody could misunderstand.

But now that the problem of the title had been solved and Signor

Pacini had been instructed to translate the libretto into French with as much logic as possible, the statutes of the Opéra came knocking at the door and majestically insisted on a hearing. A graceful giant entered and issued a command: there must be dancing. Consternation all round, for of all the many things to be discerned in the score of *Der Freischütz* there was not a single *air de danse*. Rack their brains as they would, nobody could point to a passage in this impossible music to which the gentleman in gold satin tights and the two long-legged ladies in short skirts might be asked to dance. Surely not to the common beat of the *Ländler* before Max's aria? Then perhaps after the hunters' chorus—or after Agathe's aria *'Wie nahte mir der Schlummer'*? No, it was quite hopeless. Yet somewhere they must be dancing. A ballet would have to be written into *Der Freischütz*, even though in all else it would be performed exactly as it was. Whatever pangs of conscience there may have been were soon overcome when somebody remembered that Weber himself had written an *Invitation to the Dance*. Who could possibly object if the dancing were done on the composer's own invitation? Congratulations all round: everything was now settled.

But then another giant rose up from the statutes and proclaimed: 'Thou shalt not speak!' The unhappy committee of investigation had completely forgotten that in *Der Freischütz* the singers have as much to say as they have to sing. Gloom descended once more. As everybody brooded and sighed, the opera director raised his eyes to heaven and asked what was now to become of his *Freischütz* in the original. This time there was no way out. The recitatives in *Euryanthe* did not fit, otherwise they could have been put to use in the same way as the *Invitation to the Dance*. There was no alternative but *force majeure*: the dialogue must be turned into recitative. Unfortunately no Italian was at hand to compose recitatives for a German opera; the Spaniards were momentarily showing little interest in music; and the English were too much occupied with their Corn Bill. Nothing remained therefore but to engage a Frenchman. And since Monsieur Berlioz had already written so much odd and eccentric music, it seemed to the committee that he would be just the man to supply a little extra music for this odd and original *Freischütz*.

M. Berlioz was delighted that *Der Freischütz* had fallen into his lap, for he knew it and loved it and was confident that in his hands it would suffer the minimum amount of distortion. With true artistic integrity he resolved to alter not a single note in Weber's score, to leave nothing out and to add only what the director and the committee of investigation deemed unavoidable to comply with the Opéra's tyrannical statutes. He felt that as far as possible this work should be given the same respect that we in Germany give for example to *Fra Diavolo* or *The Black Domino*, which we present in their original form without putting in Bachian fugues or eight-part motets or omitting such witty couplets as '*So schön und froh, Postillon von Longjumeau*'.

Although it was comforting to know that our beloved *Freischütz* had come into the best of French hands, namely M. Berlioz's, I still could not help feeling certain misgivings in my German heart. I simply could not believe that a people that found it impossible to present our *Freischütz* in its opera house in its original form would be able to understand and appreciate it at all, particularly in so outwardly distorted a shape. I therefore decided in my patriotic zeal to give the Paris public the benefit of my views on the enterprise, and I wrote and published an article in which I spoke both freely and frankly. I defined the nature of *Der Freischütz* and described the saga on which it is based in considerable detail, and I tried to explain as clearly as possible what we mean by a *franc-tireur*, what we think about a *balle franche* and what significance we attach to a bridal wreath. In other words, I tried to familiarise my French readers with all the notions that German children imbibe with their mother's milk. And of course I drew their attention to Bohemian forests and the German propensity for day-dreaming. In this respect my task was not difficult, since no Frenchman can visualise a German without forests and a tendency to dream. I went on to express my misgivings that male dancers in satin tights and long-legged ladies in short skirts might have a damaging effect on the simple structure of the original work. But in particular I warned my readers to what extent the many small musical numbers—especially the very short ones—would suffer by the introduction of recitative, which would necessarily take up an undue proportion of the work and thus spoil the effect of its songs and arias; while the disappearance of the fresh and naive German dialogue would lead to a loss of colour and vitality, however good the musical treatment. In this way I did what I could to present a case for our national property *before* almost inevitable failure overtook it.

Everyone told me I was wrong: *Der Freischütz*, they said, was not as original as all that. But unfortunately practically everything I had predicted turned out to be true. After the performance some people told me that I had been right all the time. Others, however, declared roundly that our *Freischütz* was worthless. An appalling verdict, and I know for a certainty that these people are wrong. How could they ever have come to entertain the thought that *Der Freischütz* is worthless? To understand that, you would have had to see and hear this production of it in the theatre of the Académie royale de Musique.

M. Berlioz had been unable to engage the opera house's best singers for his production. He, the public and the work itself had to make do with the second best. Suffice it to say that even the best are not up to much. As for the second best, both the male and female singers are children of darkness. They very often get laughed at, and, as everyone knows, this is liable to spoil the effect of an opera, even when it is French. But in the case of our splendid *Freischütz*, much of which the French are bound by their very nature to find ridiculous, these second-rate singers might have provided entertainment, perhaps—but hardly edification. I myself laughed quite a lot, even when the French themselves were serious, for, when I at last came to the conclusion that what I was seeing was not by any stretch of the imagination my beloved *Freischütz*, I abandoned all my well-meaning scruples and laughed more madly than all the rest—except at that spot already referred to at the beginning, when I wept.

In general one might say that the whole cast at the great Paris Opéra dreamed its way through the work. For this I myself must perhaps assume part of the blame, since it was I who drew attention in my article to the German addiction to forests and day-dreaming. It appeared that my hints had been absorbed and acted upon with frightening punctiliousness. The scenic designers had of course not been sparing with their forests, and so nothing was left for the singers but to provide the dreaming. In addition, they wept a lot, and

Samiel even trembled. About Samiel's tremblings I had better speak at once, for it was these that finally overcame my scruples and enabled me to find consolation in laughter.

Samiel was a slim young man of about twenty-five. He wore a handsome Spanish costume, over which he occasionally threw a cloak of black crape. He had a highly expressive face, to which some striking side-whiskers lent even more interest. His general air was alert and cheerful, and in the first act he played the police spy with true Parisian *élan*. Body bent forward and a finger to his lips, he approached Max several times with graceful circumspection as the unhappy young hunter sang his great aria. His purpose, it seemed, was to catch what Max was singing, and that was in truth no simple matter, for even the audience, despite the help of text books, not infrequently seemed uncertain whether he was singing in Italian or French. On one occasion, at the point where Max moved up to the footlights to hurl his despairing question at the fates, Samiel drew so close that he actually heard the word *dieu*, bellowed forth with tremendous force. This word seemed to make a very unpleasant impression on him, for the moment he heard it he fell into a fit of trembling the like of which I have never seen before, even in the French theatre. It is of course well known that in the art of trembling French actors and actresses are unrivalled throughout the world, but what Samiel achieved on this occasion made all previous efforts look like child's play. The stage of the Paris Opéra is, as you may imagine, very broad and deep, so you can appreciate what a huge distance poor Samiel had to cover when, from Max's position at the extreme left of front, he had to make his escape with violently trembling limbs all the way to the extreme right at back. Pursuing his shaky course, he had still, some time later, only reached the middle of the stage, and, in view of the tremendous exertion this manoeuvre had so far cost him, one began to fear that he would never be able to make his distant goal at the back. However, on French stages nothing is ever left to chance. The producer had reckoned at what point in his journey Samiel's powers would give out, and he had arranged with the stage technicians to whisk him away through a trap door. All went according to plan, though only in the nick of time. A flash of lightning over the place where he had been standing completed the effect. We were left with the comforting feeling that the godless man would be given time and treatment in his subterranean dwelling to recover from the exhausting effects of all that trembling.

Max elected to emphasise the dreamy side of his character. Though this suited the part as a whole well enough, he tended on occasions to push his dreamy forgetfulness too far. Frequently he forgot the key in which Weber in his wisdom had directed the orchestra to play and, lost in his dreams, sang in a somewhat lower one, with an effect that was strange, certainly, but not very pleasing. In his aria he strayed about in sad confusion between the forests and the meadows. One might say that he overdid the dreamy confusion as well as the mood of flatness that assailed him.

His friend Kaspar, on the other hand, seemed both cheerful and carefree, although there was something very odd about his appearance: his good-humoured behaviour was in striking contrast with the lugubrious expression on his face, and nothing could have been more melancholy than his manner of walking. The singer playing Kaspar has hitherto shown his laudable public spirit by singing in the chorus—this notwithstanding that he is unusually tall. However, moved by a proper concern for appearances, he has always done his utmost to bring his towering limbs into a seemly relationship with the more modest proportions of his colleagues. Since nothing could be done to his head end without considerable inconvenience to himself, he chose the alternative remedy of reducing his body to an acceptable length by bending his legs both downwards and outwards at the knee. Such self-sacrifice has always—or nearly always—enabled the chorus to maintain an excellent ensemble, and on this occasion his unselfish behaviour proved equally advantageous for the part of the blackly villainous Kaspar. In conjunction with the lugubrious expression on his face, it provided an effective counterbalance for the actor's own inborn air of *bonhomie*. At least, this was how it appeared to the French. However funny they found Kaspar's facial expression and his walk, they were convinced that this was how it was meant to be: the singer, they felt, was simply doing his best to comply faithfully with the demands of his role. But towards the end of the opera even they began to realise that Kaspar was in league with the devil. How in fact could they have doubted it after witnessing the strange death—or rather burial—of the godless fellow? After Kaspar is struck down by that incomprehensible bullet—incomprehensible to the French, that is, owing to its lack of logic—he is, as you will remember, visited once more by Samiel. As villains usually do, he curses both God and the world. But he so far forgets himself as to honour Samiel himself with a curse, and on this occasion the latter was so incensed that he straight away carried the impudent fellow off beneath the stage instead of leaving his corpse lying there. This proved a great embarrassment to the chorus, who still had some words to say to Kaspar, and it also disconcerted the prince who, as we all know, had formed the intention of throwing the corpse into the Wolf's Glen. However, both prince and chorus solved the difficulty with true French presence of mind by carrying on as if nothing unusual had happened, taking their revenge following Kaspar's premature departure by reviling him in his absence.

The prince and his court, incidentally, were seen to be richly deserving of respect. All were dressed in oriental costume, and one got the impression that the prince's rule extended over an empire of truly vast dimensions. He himself, together with some of his nobles, wore Turkish dress, suggesting that he must be the sultan or at least a pasha of Egypt. The rest of the court, including the very large bodyguard, wore Chinese costumes—thus proving that their master's domain stretched at the very least from Constantinople to Peking. Since everybody else was properly and accurately dressed in the costume of Bohemia, one was bound to assume that the mighty sultan had also extended his territories north-westwards to Prague and Töplitz. Now, since everyone knows that even at the height of their glory the Turks never advanced further than the outskirts of Vienna, we are obliged to conclude, either that the costume designer of the Paris Opéra is in possession of historical documents which enable him to know more about the exploits of the Turks than the rest of us or that, consciously or unconsciously, he had switched the action of our *Freischütz* from Bohemia to Hungary. True, this assumption was not supported by the costumes of the hunters and peasants, which were unmistakably Bohemian and not Hungarian, but it does have historical fact in its favour, since Hungary did once belong to the Turkish sultan. The idea is anyway romantic, not to say exotic. In any case it was salutary to see the ruler of all the Mussulmans so magnanimously engaged in Christian negotiations with a hermit. It was a lesson to all Christian nations that Moslems and Jews should also be treated as normal human beings.

However, let us now put these production details aside. If I were to spell out all the things which turned my patriotic dismay into helpless laughter, I should have a large but also very exhausting task on my hands. Let me therefore now confine my remarks simply to the interpretation of our *Freischütz* in Paris in terms of the production as a whole.

Quite apart from my misgivings over the disproportionate length of the specially composed recitatives, I had felt some initial fears that M. Berlioz might be tempted, where opportunity offered, to yield to the impetuosity of his own inspiration and thus to give his recitatives too much independence. But—much to my regret, I am amazed to find myself saying—M. Berlioz renounced all personal ambition and did his utmost to make his work as unobtrusive as possible. The reason for my regret was that *Der Freischütz*, besides being inevitably distorted, also became unbearably boring. This was particularly unfortunate in view of the fact that it was solely for the benefit of the French audience that M. Berlioz's work had been done. Of course it would have set our German teeth on edge to have had to listen to the outbursts of applause which M. Berlioz's recitatives would certainly have aroused if he had abandoned his modesty and given way to his own ambitious inspirations. But, from the point of view of its production in Paris, this applause would have been to the advantage of *Der Freischütz* itself, for the French would have felt entertained and would not have finished up by condemning the work of our fellow-countryman as a bore. That is in fact exactly what happened: these recitatives robbed Weber's romantic opera of its freshness and integrity, but offered nothing in their place. They were to a large extent responsible for the audience's despair, for they opened the gates to that most terrible of all torments—utter boredom.

The way in which they were sung also helped to emphasise the reprehensible nature of these recitatives. All the singers seemed to imagine that they were singing *Norma* or *Moses* and treated us to portamentos, tremolos and other such noble devices.

These became most painfully evident in the scenes between the two girls, Agathe and Ännchen. Agathe obviously saw herself throughout as Donizetti's *Favorita*—the wronged innocent—and so she wept a great deal, maintained a look of set gloom and was prone to sudden paroxysms of fear. She had been given a Bohemian peasant costume to wear, all velvet and lace. It was at least in character, whereas Ännchen was clad in a coquettish evening gown. This lady seemed dimly to realise that she was supposed to be a skittish creature, but skittishness is as foreign to French women as coquetry is to ours. The silliest of Ännchens to be seen on our German stages will, when she sings about handsome boys, take the two corners of her apron in her hands and trip towards Agathe. She will nod her head at appropriate moments and drop her eyes when it is called for. But our Paris Ännchen could do none of these things. She elected to stay rooted to one spot and to flirt with the 'Lions' in their boxes, thereby imagining that she was doing all that was necessary to depict a German girl. The Parisians did not seem to find this in any way remarkable—and nor did I.

But the scene in which the Paris Opéra's disastrous ban on spoken dialogue wreaked the most havoc was the Wolf's Glen. All the words which Weber directed to be spoken in this melodrama by Kaspar and Max had of course to be sung, and this stretched things out to unbearable lengths. It was this factor that most of all incensed the French. They considered this 'devil's kitchen', as they called it, an incomprehensibly stupid affair anyway, and to see so much time spent on it tried their patience beyond endurance. Maybe if they had been given something intriguing to look at—a chain of imps and sylphides instead of boring skulls, a luscious ballerina flashing her skirts and legs instead of an indolent owl stretching its wings, or a bevy of liberal-minded nuns attempting to seduce the phlegmatic young hunter—if any of these things had happened, then the Paris audience would at least have known where they were. But none of them did, and even Kaspar, who should have been mainly occupied with the task of casting his bullets, seemed to be bothered by the extraordinary lack of happenings. I was in no better state myself. Becoming increasingly aware of the audience's restlessness around me, I found myself silently praying to all the saints in heaven that the stage manager might at last feel the urge to produce something from his box of tricks.

Thus it was that both Kaspar and I, after the first bullet had been cast, responded with undisguised delight to the sound of a sudden unexpected rustling in one of the bushes. But whatever had caused it vanished with the speed of lightning, leaving nothing unfortunately but a very unpleasant smell behind. However, this served to raise our hopes initially, though with the second bullet they remained unfulfilled. Expectantly Kaspar called up the third bullet, and I waited with him, agog. Again nothing happened. We were ashamed by Samiel's inactivity and hung our heads. But only for a moment, for the fourth bullet had to be cast. This time we were gratified to see, beside a couple of bats flying above the circle, a number of will-o'-the-wisps dancing in the air. Unfortunately they got too close to the melancholy Max, who was obviously put out by them. Still, we could now await the casting of the fifth bullet with the most sanguine expectations: if the ghostly wild chase was to be shown, it was now or never. And sure enough, it came. On a mountain, six feet above the heads of the two hunters, we saw four naked boys, bathed in a mysterious light. They were carrying bows and arrows, and for this reason were generally taken to be cupids. They made a few gestures in cancan style and then hurried off into the wings. Much the same thing was then done by a lion, a bear and a wolf, as well as by four more boys who, naked and armed with bows and arrows, likewise followed in the wild hunters' wake.

Alarming as these apparitions had been, both Kaspar and myself would have liked them to continue after the sixth bullet. But at this point the producer prudently opted for a respite—no doubt in order to allow the ladies in their boxes to recover a little from their fright. When, after the casting of the seventh bullet, I saw what transpired, I understood the reason for this pause in the proceedings. Without it the intended spine-chilling effect could never have been achieved. On the bridge across the waterfall three men appeared, dressed in striking black cloaks. Three more appeared in the foreground on the very spot where Max was standing. He must, I suppose, have taken them for undertakers. At any rate, they made such a ghastly impression on him that he immediately fell down full length at their feet. The horrors of the Wolf's Glen were at an end.

I see I have once more relapsed into a catalogue of details. In order to block up this tempting path once and for all, I shall resolve to say not a word more about the production of *Der Freischütz* in Paris, but instead to concentrate my attention upon the public and its reaction to our national work.

Most Parisians tend to think of productions at the Paris Opéra as being above reproach, which is not surprising, since they know of no other establishment where they might see an opera better performed. Thus they were bound to feel that this production of *Der Freischütz* was good all through—certainly better than anything they could have seen in a German theatre. Instead of attributing those aspects of *Der Freischütz* which they found boring and silly to the shortcomings of the performance—this would never have entered their heads— they simply concluded that what the Germans took to be a master- piece was, so far as they were concerned, just a piece of clumsy hack- work. And this opinion was confirmed by their recollection of *Robin des Bois*, that adaptation of *Der Freischütz* which, as I have already said more than once, had been a tremendous success. Since the work on which it was based had failed to match its success, everybody not unnaturally formed the opinion that the adaptation was incompar- ably the better work. Certainly in *Robin des Bois* the effect of Weber's music had not been spoiled by M. Berlioz's terribly long recitatives, and it had had the additional advantage that the author had con- trived to introduce *logic* into the dramatic action.

This logic is a very remarkable thing. Not only have the French constructed their language according to the strictest rules of logic, but they also demand that everything said in it should be logical too. I have met Frenchmen who found a lot of pleasure even in this pro- duction of *Der Freischütz*, but every one of them complained that the work lacks logic. I have never in my whole life felt constrained to examine *Der Freischütz* for its logical content, and I therefore asked these Frenchmen to explain exactly what they meant by it. Thus I learned that logical French brains were particularly vexed by the *number* of magic bullets. Why, they asked, were there seven? Was such luxury really necessary? Would not three have done? Three is a number that can always be controlled and managed. How is it possible in one short act to put seven whole bullets to really practical use? One would need at least five complete acts to solve this problem properly, and even then one would be faced with the difficulty of finding a use for more than one bullet in a single act. They were prepared to admit that handling magic bullets is no laughing matter; but in that case was it not a defiance of all reason that two young hunters should shoot off six of them with such glaring irresponsibility, particularly when they knew, as they must have done, that the seventh bullet held an unpleasant surprise in store?

In the same way the catastrophe at the end was mercilessly criticised. 'How is it possible', I was asked, 'that a shot fired at a dove should appear to kill a bride and actually kill a good-for-nothing hunter at one and the same time? Granted, a shot can miss a dove and hit a human being—such unfortunate accidents do happen. But that a bride and all around her should imagine for a full five minutes that *she* had been hit as well—that is really going beyond the bounds of credibility. And in any case, this shot is dramatically so unconvincing. How much more logical it would be if the young hunter, in despair at having missed his mark, were to try to put the seventh magic bullet through his own head! The bride rushes in and tries to wrest the pistol from him. In the struggle it goes off, missing the hunter (thanks to the bride's intervention) and laying low his godless comrade, who happens to be standing in the direct line of fire. Now that would be *logical*!'

I clutched my reeling head. Such obvious truths had never once entered my thoughts: I had always taken *Der Freischütz* in all its illogical entirety exactly as it was. Does that not show what remarkable people the French are? They see *Der Freischütz* once only, and immediately they can demonstrate that for twenty-five years we Germans have been labouring under a monstrous delusion regarding its logicality. What fools we must be, to have always believed without question that a shot fired at an eagle at seven o'clock in the evening could cause the portrait of a great-grandfather to fall from the wall in a hunting lodge half a mile away!

Logic is the Frenchman's consuming passion, and consequently it informs all their judgments. However conflicting the newspaper reports, none of them neglected in this case to base their opinions on

the most logical premises, even if this must often have proved difficult. One paper maintained, for instance, that the marksman was
wearing grey, whereas another thought his costume was unmistakably green. But it was M. Berlioz in the *Journal des Débats* who
contrived things best. In his article on *Der Freischütz* he did not
neglect to say nice things about both Weber and his masterpiece,
and his words were all the more telling in that he was equally nice
about the production. Nobody objected to that of course, for we all
knew that the writer had himself been responsible for the musical
mise en scène, and he was consequently under an obligation to compliment the singers for the trouble they had gone to in studying so
disagreeable an opera under his care. But M. Berlioz's true modesty
was revealed by the fact that in his article he said not a single word
about his recitatives. Thus everyone was touched when, in an ensuing issue of the journal, M. Berlioz's colleague, Jules Janin, graciously
took the trouble of reviewing the *Freischütz* production himself and
found occasion to praise only one thing about it: the recitatives of his
friend, M. Berlioz. There was nobody who did not feel that this divi-
sion of labour between the two colleagues was completely in line
with the principles of Parisian logic.

Other journals reacted differently according to their own special
brand of logic. Those in opposition to the Paris Opéra and its director
naturally could not desist from condemning the production absolutely,
and these sought to strengthen their case further by tearing our
Freischütz to bits into the bargain.

But the most logical expression of all was to be found in *Charivari*.
There the writer found fit to congratulate the Paris Opéra for having
*granted asylum to this masterpiece from Germany after it had been dis-
avowed by its composer's own fellow-countrymen and banned from performance on its native soil.*

Having come this far, my patience now finally gave out. Up to
this point I had laughed, and could find plenty to laugh at in the
article in *Charivari* too. But there is a point at which laughter stops,
however much cause for it may still remain. If I were to tell you,
my German fellow-countrymen, what it was that made me decide
not to laugh over this last item, then you would learn that it was my
anger at being denied, in the great capital of an ostentatiously free

France, the opportunity of replying forcefully to this idiotic libel—
or indeed of finding space in any journal to expose the deficiencies of
this Parisian *Freischütz*! The French, you must understand, permit
attacks and denials only between warring parties, and in such cases
feel no qualms over accusing their opponents of lack of understanding
or even of honour. But any statement or explanation, however calm
and reasonable, that is addressed to *all* parties must never be allowed
to reach their ears. In such cases they mutually swap lies about what
they know and what they do not know, make copious use of their
dubious logic and take pride in knowing nothing about anything
except what they *want* to know.

Well, that is the way they are. These intellectual Frenchmen lack
not only the ability but also the will, even for the sake of curiosity, to
step beyond the boundaries of their traditional conceptions of good
and evil. In saying that I have said nothing new. There is in any case
nothing new to be said about them, for, in spite of their ever changing
fashions, they themselves can never change. But I feel I must draw
your attention again to what has been said so often before, since in
recent times the impression has been forming among us that a
rapprochement is now taking place between the Germans and the
French, particularly in matters of art. No doubt this feeling is due,
as far as we are concerned, to the knowledge that the French have
been translating Goethe and play Beethoven's symphonies excellently
well. It is true that both these things have happened and are happening. But, as I have now told you, they are also performing *Der
Freischütz*. What this work has done to bring the two nations closer
together Goethe and Beethoven have also done—no more. And this
is less than little, for *Der Freischütz* has really succeeded only in
driving the French and the Germans farther apart again.

On this matter we should be under no illusions: in many ways the
French will always be strangers to us, though we may all wear the
same suits and cravats.

If, for any of a thousand reasons we may justifiably have, we wish
to come closer to them, we shall be obliged to surrender a good proportion of our own best national characteristics. It is not possible
to deceive the French. No external factors can persuade them that
we are making French music, for instance, unless the whole inner

approach is modelled on what they call their logic. It is hard work, and anyone speaking from experience can assure you that an extra strong dose of national feeling and patriotism is needed to preserve one's core intact against all that the French demand of one. And for this reason there is no more delicious feeling than the consciousness of occasionally managing to fool the French along with all their abundant logic. But it is not easy, for no one has sharper eyes than they, and their customs barriers are designed with extraordinary severity to deny entry to all foreign goods. Or at any rate the entry fee is enormous and troublesome to raise.

How over-honest and indulgent we Germans are by comparison, in the way we pick over the vaunted masterpieces of our neighbours with such busy concern in our search for tasty morsels! We even accept the nasty-tasting bits as something unusual and foreign and bear them off to the chemist to be made into medicine, with which we hope to cure our digestions, ruined by too much sitting. It never seems to occur to us that these preparations may not be effective against anything, except perhaps bugs and fleas. The Parisian, however, knows his own goods so thoroughly that he does not even trust them for *that* purpose, whence it comes that the pests in France's glorious capital proliferate so hugely.

Oh, how kind you are, my German friends, towards all the wretched things which even the French themselves find disgusting! But do you know that this angelic virtue of yours makes you a laughing-stock among these gay people? Do you know what they say to make you look ridiculous in the eyes of Parisian society? They say you went to the opera in Berlin or Vienna in April or May of this year to see either *Fra Diavolo* or *Zampa*. Every Frenchman who hears this decides, on the strength of his logic, that you must be the most undiscriminating people on earth, and splits his sides laughing.

I was recently in a place where I heard this kind of superior laughter. Since I had just finished laughing rather too much over other things, I did not join in now, but clenched my fists and swore an oath. If there is anyone who cares to know what I swore, he will learn about it in time. *If I were more than I am, if I were one of those indomitable heroes of whom Schiller writes in his hexameters, then you*

would learn at once what it was I swore when I heard the French laughing
at our piety towards Zampa *and* Fra Diavolo.

That we, a very gifted people to whom God presented a Mozart
and a Beethoven, should be thought to exist merely for the purpose
of giving the Paris salons something to laugh at! For that is what we
serve for now—and we deserve it. The shallowest head on the
Boulevard des Italiens has the right to laugh at us, because we ask for
it. I make no reproaches for our ability to recognise the good points
of French art: it is this very quality that raises us head and shoulders
over the French themselves. It is to our credit that we are able to
appreciate everything other countries offer us down to the last drop.
This gift, vouchsafed us Germans by a bountiful heaven, is to be
highly prized, for without it a universal genius such as Mozart would
never have risen among us, and because of it we are able to forgive
the mockery of all those who like to laugh at us. But all the same it is
a law of nature that there should be times of war as of peace. So, if in
times of war you feel like taking revenge on the French, there would
be no more exquisite way of punishing them than by sending the
emissaries of their holy spirit—*Fra Diavolo, Zampa, Le fidèle Berger*
and whatever else they may be called—back to them by special
delivery. You can rest assured that, if the French were forced to
listen to the sermons of these inspired teachers once again, they
would die of boredom, for the French are above all things a witty
people and, if there is one thing they really cannot bear, it is *ennui*.

This, my fellow Germans, would be a fine and well-deserved
punishment for the ill-treatment to which our cherished *Freischütz*
has been subjected here. If you have really banished it from your soil,
as *Charivari* so confidently asserts, then do, I beg you, take it back
again. You have plenty of worse goods to offer which the French
would be delighted to accept in exchange for your *Freischütz*.

Wonders from Abroad

(Report to the Dresden *Abendzeitung*)

6 July 1841

They have not been able to kill it—our dear and wonderful Freischütz! They did all they could humanly and legally do: they made it boring, they left it in all its illogicality, they played with it all those tricks which I recently described to my readers in the *Abendzeitung* and which I do not intend to repeat again—*and still they were unable to kill it!* It is given evening after evening, the public streams to it in ever increasing numbers, grows more and more enthusiastic and shouts *bis!* wherever it possibly can. At first I was uncertain whether I should pay tribute for this happy outcome to the Paris public or to *Der Freischütz* itself. I even thought the production might have had something to do with it: perhaps it had now undergone a change for the better. But no, everything was just as before: the same dreaming, weeping and trembling, the same 'horrors' in the Wolf's Glen, the same unselfseeking joviality on the part of Kaspar. In the end I came to the conclusion that on the whole it was *Der Freischütz* which deserved praise rather than the Paris public.

All the same, the public, by having the courage in spite of those terrible first performances to repair once more to the red plush benches of the Opéra and listen to *Der Freischütz* again from beginning to end, provided evidence of its strength, patience and extraordinary elasticity. In such circumstances the work was bound eventually to fight free of all its tiresome trappings and reveal itself as it really is—young, fresh and splendid.

But wait: I am going too far. Young, fresh and splendid, *as it really is*—these are qualities which it could never reveal to the people of Paris. The very things we Germans so cherish in it could not in a thousand years hope to appeal to the hearts of the Parisians: French custom forbids it. But on the other hand the French detect in *Der Freischütz* beauties which we Germans virtually ignore, or at least take happily for granted. I am speaking of its purely musical beauties and its many wonderful effects, achieved with an unpretentious modesty that represents something entirely new to the French and arouses their unfeigned enthusiasm. It is impossible to imagine how enraptured they are, for example, by that lovely B major passage in the concluding finale, despite the fact that they regard the whole extended final scene with the venerable hermit as an abomination. The few bars in this passage where all the solo voices are singing together arouses in them a tremendous response. To the credit of the Parisians I can say that I have never heard them greet even Rubini's most thrilling cadence more enthusiastically. They shout for an encore, in spite of the fact that Berlioz earnestly begged them in the *Journal des Débats* to keep silent after this passage, in order not to obscure the point at which the hermit modulates so beautifully into C major. Heavens alive, what do the Parisians care about hermits— especially when modulating into C major?

What is chiefly responsible for this happy and unexpected success of *Der Freischütz* is the tremendous reputation enjoyed by the German masterpiece. Presented as it first was in Paris, what chance would it have stood if it had been the work of some unknown composer? Both it and its creator would have been sunk without trace and no musical dictionary anywhere in the world would have registered even the name of the composer. *Charivari* would have commented on its success in the same way that it described the reception of Berlioz's *Benvenuto Cellini*: 'The audience went to sleep and awoke hissing.' A witty remark certainly, but once is enough! Anyway, here no such remark was called for: the public must have received some confused sort of impression at that wretched first performance of *Der Freischütz's* true quality, otherwise it would not have felt so baffling a desire to hear it again. However, as I have already said, that was as far as it was prepared to go: *Der Freischütz* itself had to do the rest. *And this it did:* people are flocking in, clapping and cheering. Ah, wonderful *Freischütz*! There is even talk of some act of generosity towards the German master's heirs. Well, we shall see!

And now we have had a German ballet as well. It is set, or rather danced, in Silesia, not far from Breslau, and a German poet, Heinrich Heine, provided the idea for it. This is the saga of the Willis— maidens who died of thwarted love and now rise from their graves at midnight in order to dance all men who approach them to their deaths. It was this legend's suitability for balletic treatment that particularly attracted the French, and indeed what better opportunity could be provided for fabulous pirouettes and ravishing *entrechats* than the Willis and their mysterious urge? To make these death-dances more convincing the adapter has very rightly chosen to set his scene near Breslau, rather than in Paris, for only when they are able to regard the victims of the dance as Germans can the French be persuaded to take them seriously. As every spectator at masked balls in Paris can see for himself, no Frenchman has ever been danced to death, or ever will be.

The character, habits and qualities of the French make many things unthinkable or incomprehensible to them, particularly in the realm of poetry. It is for this reason that opera and ballet librettists often feel obliged to seek their wonders abroad, which not only gives them the choice of a thousand peculiar happenings but also enables them to demand unconditional belief from their public. If the foreign wonder is presented, as is now very much the fashion, under a foreign name, then so much the better: in a *Franc-tireur* the French would have found plenty to object to, but they are quite happy with *Le Freischutz*, which is for them synonymous with the back of beyond. For the same reason the title *Les Willis* is equally unobjectionable: if these Willis do actually find men who can dance themselves to death, difficult though this may be to visualise, presumably such unusual and badly organised creatures must really exist somewhere. 'What extraordinary places', they think, 'Silesia, Thuringia and the lands around them must be!' We Germans have no need of the Willis: one single Paris Opéra Ball is quite enough for us.

Incidentally, this ballet is like all the rest: good dancing, beautiful scenery, agreeable music. This time the music is provided by M. Adam, the man who wrote *Le Postillon de Longjumeau*. This composer has burnt himself out with disgraceful rapidity—written himself to death in almost as short a time as the victim of the Willis danced himself to death. But M. Adam's case the French can easily understand: they see composers dying of their own music every few months and are always ready to help bury them. Now and again they learn that the departed soul is still peddling his music in Germany. No wonder they consider Germany to be a land of spectres and spooks!

M. Adam, however, is still haunting Paris. Month by month he is just on the point of being forgotten for ever when he turns up again. With *Les Willis* too he timed his appearance to coincide with his departure: he is always just on the point of leaving—tomorrow for St Petersburg or Berlin, the day after for Constantinople—to toss off a little ballet for the sum of 100,000 francs. A truly remarkable spectre!

A young Alsatian composer and scholar, Johann Kastner, has also put in an appearance (his first) at the Opéra comique. Known up till now—at least in Paris—mainly as a resourceful teacher, he sought an opportunity to display his talents as a dramatic composer—an opportunity which, in view of his very favourable family circumstances, was not unduly difficult to find. However, owing to the horrible habit prevailing in Parisian theatres, he was more or less forced to accept the first libretto the Opéra comique offered him. A free choice or a voluntary collaboration with a poet would anyway have been out of the question, since Paris provides neither choice nor poets. And in any case the opera directors are so accustomed to the purely routine nature of their business that they would be quite unable to grasp what free choice and poetical collaboration means, even if these were available. Herr Kastner was given so embarrassingly threadbare and unworthy a libretto that he probably did not know what to do with it and therefore wrote a whole succession of fugues. That at any rate is how it seemed to the audience, who claimed during the performance of *La Maschera* to have heard nothing but fugues from beginning to end. These the docile patrons of the Opéra comique found anything but agreeable, and they complained of a breach in the terms of their subscription contract: they had not entered into any obligation to listen to Handel. My own feeling was that the music contained many fine passages, yet I think Herr Kastner would be well advised to leave dramatic music alone and concentrate his attention on a genre more suited to the somewhat passionless rigidity of his musical talents. In this strict style of composition Herr Kastner constitutes a praiseworthy exception among the vast composer-population of Paris.

The same theatre recently brought out a very charming new trifle entitled *Les deux Voleurs,* with music by the conductor of the Opéra comique orchestra, M. Girard. In this opera various diamonds and a gold watch were stolen with much elegance and circumspection. So the little piece was quite rewarding, particularly since the stealing was done so realistically that it had all the members of the audience involuntarily feeling for their own diamonds and gold watches—all, that is, except me.

But what are all these novelties compared with the tremendous calamity which now afflicts Paris? I am not speaking of the quiet season, the departure of all political notabilities, the somersaults of M. Sauzet, the shocking price of beef and veal, the awful deficit in the state budget, the dreadful taxes imposed in favour of the fortifications, the threat of impending revolution. No, it is none of these things, but a quite different, tremendous misfortune that has struck the pitiful inhabitants of Paris, emptied the elegant *Quartiers* with a single stroke, transformed the Faubourg du Roule and the Faubourg St Germain into villages, caused grass to grow between the paving-stones of the Chaussée d'Antin and turned its mansions into a resting-place for owls! Those glorious mansions—ah, how I pity them! How deeply I feel for their former perfumed and satin-clad occupants! And why? *Because Rubini is going, never to return!* With a genial smile and gentle but iron resolution the great man has decided for the last time to confer the blessing of his presence upon his friends in fiery Spain and cold Russia and then proceed via Berlin to Italy, the land of his fathers. And thereafter he will not, as I say, return to Paris. There is depression everywhere: the cobbler throws away his awl, the tailor his needle, the milliner smashes her hat-blocks, the *parfumier* scatters his fragrances to all the winds; no more orders for silk will be despatched to Lyon, no more requests for ribbons written to Lille; for, alas, the tender guests of the Italian Opera will be wearing hair shirts in place of silk, girdling themselves with rope and not with ribbons; they will scatter ashes, not perfumes, on their heads and go about with beggarly sandals in place of satin shoes; for Rubini—*Rubini,* who was the reason for it all—will come no more. I cannot understand Louis Philippe: it *must* lead to revolution. Surely he has enough power to make Rubini stay?

Tout s'en va! But what can one do?

I see that Germany has been reading other sad news from Paris. Much is being written about an embarrassing affair concerning the poet Heinrich Heine. It seems that everyone is delighted with what has happened and on top of that claims the right to express fairly clearly the conviction that Heine deserved no better treatment than that recently meted out to him here. [*Editorial note:* Heine, who lived in Paris, had published an insulting insinuation in one of his books, and the angry victim was reported to have struck him in public. According to a report in the *Leipziger Allgemeine Zeitung,* Heine made no effort to retaliate.]

One must admit that we Germans are a magnanimous people. We see a talent arising in our midst such as Germany has few to show; its freshness and wit delights us and we shout 'Bravo' as we watch its possessor rousing our young spirits out of their state of lethargy, blazing with his great gifts the trail which the unborn creators of our future literature must follow to reach their new and unknown goal. Whenever a young German takes up his pen, he attempts—successfully or unsuccessfully, consciously or unconsciously—to imitate Heine, for never before has a style, emerging so suddenly and with the unexpectedness of a lightning flash, dominated the scene so irresistibly. Not enough, however, that we look on unprotesting when our police chase this splendid talent off its native heath; that we quickly stifle our qualms of conscience at the sight of its luxuriant roots being torn from the only soil that can nourish them; not enough that we then remark with a yawn that friend Heine has forgotten in Paris how to write travel books; that with our indifference we undermine his own delight in his talent and force him to stop being a German without the possibility of ever becoming a Parisian; not enough that we restrict his territory to such an extent that nothing is left for this superabundant mind to exercise its wits on but a few ridiculous morsels which somebody (probably inadvertently) has left behind;

not enough that we pusillanimously and *indifferently* suffer this mutilation of a talent which, more happily treated, would have become one of the greatest names in our literature. No, all this is not enough: we must also cheer and clap our hands when this same Heine is dealt with in a manner which we are more accustomed to employ against hack reviewers. And this is done in Germany with so much shameless invective that one is not given a moment to examine the true facts behind the unfortunate incident which is so eagerly regarded as a deserved punishment. The writer of that unwarrantable report in the *Leipziger Allgemeine Zeitung* has, as I can assure you, based his account of the circumstances and indeed his whole description of the incident solely on statements made by the aggressor, and his presumptuousness is in no way made more palatable by the splendid 'moral lessons' he seeks to pile on Heine's head. It has apparently occurred to nobody to seek Heine's own opinion on a matter which in any case was observed by no competent witnesses. I therefore appeal to my compatriot's sense of justice and ask them whether it is not disgraceful to condemn one party to a dispute on the sole evidence of the other?

Heine is at this moment staying at a spa in the Pyrenees and is desperately ill. If he really had not the courage to avenge a shameful insult, we must *pity* him; none of us, however, has the right to *despise* him, except perhaps the officers in our armies and the student organisations in our universities—but neither of these have anything to do with Heine.

This much is certain: the French, who would in any case have taken more care of their poet, would in similar circumstances have behaved better, even though they have their share of witty people who would have seized on a scandal of this sort as material for their ephemeral jokes. But they would not have *vilified* their poet, particularly without hearing his side of the story. I have no reason to be infatuated with the French; in this case however I prefer to take my example from them.

A First Night at the Opéra

(*La Reine de Chypre* by Halévy)

What a momentous occasion the production of a big new French opera on the Parisian stage inevitably is! Everything is in a state of turmoil. Passions are roused: envy vies with enthusiasm, curiosity with speculation, aesthetic with business considerations—all tossing and turning in a maelstrom of tears, laughs and yawns, calculations, hopes and fears! Leaving aside the librettist, the composer, the designers, the stage technicians, the ballet-master, the dancers, the singers, even the audience, we are still bound to stumble over the opera director himself. What does this first performance not signify to him! It has cost him all of forty thousand francs to mount the work, and so he is obviously on tenterhooks: will it bring him in a profit—or will he lose his whole stake at a single blow? If he has never before been in the habit of biting his fingernails, it would be humanly understandable and excusable if he were now, in the third scene of the fourth act, involuntarily to start doing so.

Who is *that* man with the black hair, anxiously peering from side to side? Apprehensive and enthusiastic at one and the same time, he searches his neighbour's face for his reaction to the last aria, while in the same instant loudly extolling its splendid theme. This is none other than the music publisher, who has already paid the composer an advance of thirty thousand francs for the score. And do you see that young musician there, with the pale face and the hungry expression in his eyes? He is listening to the performance with anxious concern, greedily snapping up the success of every single number. Is that enthusiasm or envy? It is neither, alas—but a concern for his daily bread: if the new opera catches on, he can hope for a commission from the publisher to arrange fantasies and *airs variés* on its 'favourite melodies'.

That man up in the highest corner of the gallery with his ear cupped in his hand has the task of providing the countless barrel-organs in the city with popular titbits: he is just noting down the aria of the dying king. And over there you see the representatives and plenipotentiaries of the various provincial opera managements: they are intently studying the staging of the great wedding procession and trying to distinguish how much applause is coming from the paid applauders and how much from the enthusiastic amateurs.

Far ahead in the hazy distance my homesick gaze espies—silhouetted against the romantic stage twilight of oak-groves and Italian cellars—some earnest men in black suits and brown overcoats, importantly cogitating with opera-glasses pressed firmly to their tired eyes. Who are they? Are they perhaps ruefully deploring the dilatoriness of the German and French governments, which have so far neglected to lay down railway lines leading directly from all parts of Germany to the stalls of the Paris Opéra—thus providing immediate access to the things that bring them salvation: that is to say, brand-new French operas? Ah yes, I know you! Hastily counting, I come on a total of fifty-two. You are German theatre directors!

All hail to you, illustrious beings! You have transported me back to my beloved fatherland, and that from a place more than a thousand miles away—so far, so infinitely far away that I am assailed by fears that I shall never see it again. But you—you are the great levellers of the world. You move mountains to provide our professors with French vaudevilles. You dry up the whole free Rhine to make way for a *verre d'eau* from France. And one day you will certainly build railway lines to transport big French operas, complete with wedding processions, flying dancers, palaces and machines, at one go straight into your theatre storerooms. Who said that we Germans are not enterprising?

These and similar thoughts occurred to me recently when I attended the first performance of *La Reine de Chypre*. A remarkable experience! I heard *French* verses and *French* music; I saw *Venetian* daggers and spies from the Council of Ten; I breathed the heady air of *Cyprus* and felt as if I were tasting its fiery wine—yet throughout

I was haunted by the sight of one well-nourished and grinning face among those fifty-two. Was it the shining brilliantined black hair of this spectre that compelled my involuntary attention, or was it that he appeared to be calling to me, with a triumphant expression on his face, that he would once again be the *first* to present this opera in Germany?

It was a terrible vision and even now, as I sit down to write a cool and sober report on Halévy's new opera, I cannot rid myself of it completely. My best course, it seems to me—in order to exorcise it finally—is to go straight up to that spectre with the gleaming black hair and address a few serious words to it. Why, dear ghost, do you not leave worthy people in peace when they go to the Paris Opéra to see the first production of a new work? Why do you appear at the head of those fifty-two and transport me at one stroke from Cyprus to some German trading city or other? Because I am German? Well, certainly no Frenchman would ever believe in you! But that is not good enough for me. Go away and do not let yourself be seen at the Opéra again! What has it got to do with you and your like? What business is it of yours and theirs what the Parisians write, sing, play and compose for their own people? I see your face grow long and earnest, as if you desired to convince me that you and your whole proud retinue in its silks and satins would shrivel and die if you were forced to confine yourselves to what *your* fellow-countrymen write and compose. Do you dare suggest that your fellow-countrymen have so little to offer? Why do you present no new German operas? 'Because they are so boring.' Why are they boring? 'Because our best composers never get anything but bad librettos.' So at last I get to the sore point. I dismiss the ghost and turn my thoughts to the subject of 'bad librettos', which really is a sad and sorry subject—a source of woe and despair for hundreds.

Recently a quite distinguished German composer, Herr D—, complained to me of his difficulties in finding a suitable text for an opera. He was prepared to spend money and had offered a prize for a good German libretto. Before long he received a whole number, which he read with growing disgust, then laid aside. Another composer has come here from Germany for the express purpose of acquiring, with the help of money and some diplomatic negotiations on the part of his court officials, a French libretto, which he intends to set to music after having it translated into German. I hear from Munich that the conductor Franz Lachner has at last achieved success with one of his operas, simply because the court theatre there agreed to expend 1,500 francs on ordering a libretto for him from M. de Saint-Georges. By heavens, all you poets and librettists, could your weakness be exposed more blatantly than that ? Just think for a moment: is it really so terribly difficult to write a good opera libretto ? Let me advise you how easily it can be done. The main thing is to have *poetry* inside you and your *heart* in the right place. Since you are forever reading books both new and old, you are bound one day to come on a story or event which completely grips you: you are unable to read on, because you suddenly see wonderful flesh-and-blood figures moving before your eyes, you feel their pulses throbbing, you hear their hymns of joy and their sorrowful complaints. Having come this far, what else can you possibly do but seize your pen and write down a glowing drama that must excite and shatter the emotions of every human being ? Now all you have to do is give this drama to one of those sensitive and expert musicians of whom there are always so many to be found in Germany. Your drama will then inspire *him,* and what you subsequently create together is bound to be the finest opera in the whole world.

Of course, to achieve this you will need to have a gift for poetry and emotions both deep and sensitive. Such among you as are deficient in these qualities will nevertheless possess at least *skill,* for skill is indispensable to craftsmen such as cobblers and harness-makers, and consequently to makers of librettos too. If you therefore have *skill,* read newspapers, novels and other books, and above all read the great book of *history.* You will not have to search long before you find a page or even half a page telling of some strange event which is new to you. Ponder a while over this event, draw three or even five lines across it to denote what you might call acts, and allocate to each of these acts a suitable part of the action. Make the action interesting (and there is nothing easier than that): break up a marriage here—let a lover elope with his sweetheart there—beat up a young cavalier—place a queen's crown on the head of a senator's daughter—and in the end throw the villain out of the window. Embellish all this with gold beakers containing poison, secret doors, concealed spies and other entertaining things of that sort—and in the twinkling of an eye you will have produced a libretto every bit as good as those for whose sake German composers waylay Parisian writers. Certainly you will produce one just as admirable as the text of *La Reine de Chypre*.

Should you however be so unfortunate as not to have even skill at your disposal, then do as you please—write reviews, smoke cigars, spend your evenings in bed—but do not write librettos for our poor wretched composers. For, however clever you may be in other directions, you labour under the most terrible delusions concerning this branch of your art. When you set about writing a libretto for an opera, you imagine that you must conjure up something out of the ordinary. You think you must bring on nothing but flowers and clouds instead of people—or, if you cannot get your thoughts away from people (or, more particularly, barons, officers, knights, rascals and countesses), you feel you must make them behave like clouds or flowers: otherwise it is impossible to make them *sing*. Your main concern is therefore to dispense with all action, or at least to make sure that your people do not *act* once they have been brought to the point of singing; because, according to you, music demands that everything should be *lyrical, preternaturally lyrical, indeed practically meaningless*: only then, you feel, is the composer in a position to apply the balm of his melodies and modulations. And, since it is impossible to do without action for three hours at a stretch, you see no way out of the dilemma but to make your characters tell us in good plain German speech that someone has killed someone else, that the son has found his father, but that the police have arrested everybody. To add to your troubles, you usually have the misfortune to pick on subjects which allow absolutely no scope for those splendid lyrical effusions of yours. What, for instance, does an operatic lieutenant or major say or sing when peasants threaten to thrash him? Probably nothing more than 'Good God!'—and indeed this would sound quite reasonably dramatic. But instead of that you make him sing non-sensical things about 'awful destiny' and 'divine decrees' or (when there is a woman in the neighbourhood) about 'love' and 'dove'—words which would never occur to a Prussian major in the whole of his life.

If only you could realise how much wiser you would be not to bother yourself about the composer at all, but simply to do your utmost to write, scene by scene, a real, heartfelt drama! In this way you would make it possible for him to compose some really dramatic music, instead of (as now) obstinately denying him the opportunity.

With regard to verses, it can of course be taken as a general principle that good ones are better than bad, but you would be wrong to attach too much importance to this, for often the very best of your lines are of no use at all to the composer, who may feel obliged, in order to give his music flow and expression, to hack your precious rhythms to pieces and to consign your finest rhymes to the dustbin.

To show you very clearly how, even without a gift for poetry and with only a fair measure of skill, one can construct a libretto which, in the hands of a talented composer, will interest, excite and in a certain sense satisfy an audience, let me now relate to you the plot of *La Reine de Chypre,* which was written by M. de Saint-Georges. I think it will help to prove that in this field the French are anything but bunglers.

Reading his history books, M. de Saint-Georges discovered that in the second half of the fifteenth century Venice had rapacious designs on the island of Cyprus, which was then being ruled by the Lusignan dynasty in France. The Venetians hypocritically gave their support to a prince of this dynasty, whose claims to the throne were disputed by the family. They won him the crown and then sought to strengthen their pernicious influence by marrying him off to Catarina, the daughter of a Venetian senator, Andreas Cornaro. Shortly afterwards the king died—poisoned, so it was generally supposed, by the Venetians, for on the night of his death a plot was hatched to deprive the widowed queen of her right to act as regent for their infant son. For the time being, however, the Venetian plan was foiled by Catarina's courageous resistance and her obstinate refusal to relinquish her power. This was a definite and undeniable political occurrence. Let us now see how this piece of history was used by M. de Saint-Georges as the basis of a lyrical drama in five acts.

The first act is set in Senator Andreas Cornaro's palace in Venice. Cornaro is about to present his daughter Catarina in marriage to a French cavalier, M. Duprez—or rather I should say, Gerard de

Coucy. Gerard and Catarina love each other and renew their declara-
tions in a fairly long duet. The worthy senator is pleased and gives
them his blessing. At that moment a man enters, dressed in a red robe
with a black sash: Cornaro recognises him as a member of the
Council of Ten and in alarm sends the bridal pair away. Moncenigo—
for that is the name of the disturbing visitor—informs the senator that
the Council has decided that Catarina must marry the King of Cyprus
and that Cornaro must therefore straight away revoke his promise to
the French cavalier and consent to the royal marriage, otherwise he
will pay with his life for disobeying the commands of Venice. Moncenigo grants him a few moments for reflection. While the senator is
engaged in agonised contemplation, the wedding celebrations begin.
The guests arrive—Venetian noblemen as well as French cavaliers
(Gerard's friends.) Only the senator is absent, and this provides an
opportunity for a slim and handsome young man to execute a very
well-received *pas de trois* with two of his extremely short-skirted lady
friends. This comes to an end, however, when the unhappy father
enters and announces to all present that the wedding will not take
place and that he withdraws his promise to Gerard. Everyone is
thunderstruck: questions, reproaches, complaints, threats follow one
another in quick succession. Gerard's friends accuse the senator of
breaking his word, the Venetians rally to his defence, the deceived
bridegroom rages, the poor wretched bride faints and the curtain
falls. What more could you want from a first act?

The second act takes us into Catarina's private chapel, which
needless to say provides access to the Grand Canal through wide-
open windows. The moon is shining and gondoliers are singing. The
disconsolate patrician's daughter is turning the pages of her prayer-
book, and there she finds a note from her lover, telling her that he
will come at midnight to carry her off. While she is awaiting him in
a state of blissful expectation her unhappy father enters. He begs her
forgiveness and tries, for her sake as well as his own, to win her consent to the marriage with the Cypriot king. But the more he points
out the advantages of the match, the less he succeeds in convincing
her, and he takes his leave with a heavy heart. Catarina is no sooner
left alone than the peace of her private chapel is disturbed again. She
hears her name being called. As you will have read in Victor Hugo,

that terrible Council of Ten had access to all Venetian houses of any consequence through secret doors and passages of which the occupants themselves were unaware, and this meant that their spies were able to penetrate at will into even the most heavily guarded palaces in order to carry out their foul designs. Just such a door, leading from just such a passage, is now flung wide open in the wall of the maidenly chamber, to reveal none other than Signor Moncenigo of the Council of Ten. Wasting no words, he tells the terrified patrician's daughter that, as soon as her lover arrives, she must declare that *she no longer loves him* and that she desires of her own free will to become Queen of Cyprus. Only in this way can she hope to save his life. She asks who will kill him. 'These hands!' he replies, opening the secret door to reveal a large array of assassins with drawn daggers. He then withdraws into the passage. Midnight strikes. The lover is heard approaching, but the unhappy girl cannot bring herself to hasten to his side. Just imagine what a duet this must now give rise to—the cavalier tenderly urging her to fly with him, his beloved consumed by mortal fear, watched and threatened by murderers! Reproached for her apparent coldness, she is on the point of telling him the truth: on the first occasion the awful secret door opens slightly as a warning: on the second occasion Signor Moncenigo steps through it and makes a threatening gesture, which of course she alone sees. Finally she cries out in desperation that she does not love the cavalier at all and that she wants to become a queen. Gerard's response can easily be imagined: after expressing astonishment at his beloved's gross treachery, he tells her that he now hates and despises her. She suffers terribly and appears to be on the point of collapsing. She duly does so when Gerard rushes away with an anguished cry of '*Adieu pour jamais!*' Moncenigo and the assassins then come forth and take possession of the senseless girl in order to convey her to Cyprus. This is all very Venetian and by no means uninteresting.

And now M. de Saint-Georges takes us on a free trip to Cyprus, which the third act reveals in all its glory. We are in a *casino* in Nicosia: thousands of candles illuminate the sensuous night and the stage is encircled by wonderful groves and thickets. On one side sit the gentlemen of Cyprus, on the other Venetians. Lovely voluptuous women join in the festivities, costly wines sparkle in the goblets, there is singing and dancing—one's heart leaps to see it. Signor Moncenigo is also there of course, for Venice and its Council of Ten are everywhere. And besides, there is work to do. He hears reports of the presence of a suspicious character who looks very like Gerard de Coucy, and he deems it advisable to have the unfortunate cavalier murdered at once, since here he could easily become a source of great embarrassment. After the merry throng of guests has departed, the French cavalier is heard calling for help nearby. There follows a clash of swords, until at last the assassins are routed. Gerard appears together with a strange knight, whom he thanks for having helped save him from the murderers' daggers. The stranger, who is none other than Jacques Lusignan, the King of Cyprus himself, claims only to have discharged his knightly duty, but he does not reveal his true identity, calling himself simply a subject of France. Gerard is delighted to discover a fellow countryman, and Lusignan no less so: 'Hail, thou lovely land of France!' they sing together. They swear chivalrous friendship, and with due propriety question each other. As discreetly as possible they reveal the source of their respective woes: Lusignan regards himself as an exile, forced to fight for his rights in foreign lands; Gerard admits that a great sorrow and a desire to revenge himself on those who have destroyed his happiness have led him to Cyprus. They promise to help each other, and exchange oaths of loyalty. We hear the sound of cannon shots from the harbour: the queen's ship is nearing Cyprus! Lusignan's face lights up in joy and delight: he sees his good star rising. Gerard, in whom the thunder of the cannons has aroused very different feelings, laments over the unfaithfulness of women and thirsts for revenge.

So we come to the fourth act, which is magnificently spectacular. We are at the harbour waiting with the cheering crowd for the arrival of the queen's ship. It approaches; on costly carpets she steps ashore; Lusignan, the king, comes from the palace to meet her—salvoes, pealing bells and trumpet fanfares accompany the glittering procession into the cathedral. The stage is left empty and deserted. Then the unhappy Gerard enters, brooding over his plans for vengeance. He knows they will cost him his life, yet nevertheless he is determined to enjoy his revenge before abandoning himself to a shameful death. He is about to enter the church when the returning procession drives him back. He takes up a position by the palace wall to await the king. As he approaches with Catarina at his side, Gerard rushes on him with drawn dagger. He recognises his rescuer and compatriot. Appalled, he springs back, and is seized by the guards. The crowd angrily demands his blood. The king, shocked and dismayed, reproaches him for breaking his oath: 'Me you would kill, who delivered you from the hands of assassins?' All the same he restrains the bloodthirsty mob and delivers Gerard over to the hands of Cypriot justice.

The fifth act takes place two years later. Historically the intervening period extended to four years, but M. de Saint-Georges has cleverly contrived to cut this awkwardly long interval by half. The king, grown old before his time, lies dying of a lingering sickness. Catarina, who has accepted her lot and come to respect her husband, sits at his bedside. Lusignan thanks her for her goodness and loyalty and reveals that he knows of her former relationship with Gerard: when he secretly intervened to save him from execution, Gerard in his gratitude had told him everything. The king himself, far from being angry with his wife, is filled with admiration for her loyalty and steadfastness and hopes that his fast approaching death will free her from her bonds. The arrival is announced of a hospitaller of the Knights of Malta, who has brought important messages for the king. Lusignan orders him to be brought to the queen: he feels his last hour is at hand, and he wishes his wife to assume power on behalf of their son. The knight hospitaller is received in audience by the queen, and who is he but Gerard de Coucy? This leads to a painful encounter, for old memories begin to stir. Gerard cannot resist renewing his reproaches of unfaithfulness, though Catarina is able to dispel them by revealing the terrible circumstances which had compelled her to declare that she no longer loved him. Gerard, appeased, hastens to impart his message: he has learnt from the senator, who has since died filled with remorse, that Lusignan's deadly illness is due to a poison administered by the Venetians, whom his disobedience and his unexpected show of independence have angered. Gerard has come to Cyprus in the hope of repaying Lusignan for his magnanimity by warning him of the fiendish plot and if possible saving him. 'Too late!' cries Moncenigo, who has entered unseen. 'No one can save the king now: at this very moment he is succumbing to the punishment which Venice, enraged by the defiance he dared to show, has decreed. And Venice commands you, Catarina, if you wish to retain your life, to lay the reins of government in its hands.'—'Never!' replies the queen furiously. 'I shall continue to rule on behalf of my son and to avenge my husband.'—'Who will support you in your defiance?'— 'My people, to whom I shall reveal Venice's shameful treachery.'— 'No one will believe you, for I shall say that you, in an adulterous conspiracy with this knight here, murdered your husband yourself. Who will call me a liar?'—'*I!*' It is the king himself who, not yet dead as believed, has summoned his dying strength to drag himself, pale and contorted with pain, to the door of the audience chamber, from which he hears Moncenigo's shameless words. It is a truly electrifying moment. The king declares that he will use the last remaining minutes of his life to thwart Venice's base treachery and to assure the people of his wife's innocence. The imperturbable Moncenigo makes a sign through the window with his sash. The traitor is seized by the king's guards, but it is too late: gunfire and sounds of uproar are heard. Soldiers rush out to suppress the Venetian rebellion; Gerard, glad of an opportunity to serve Lusignan, drives the Venetians from the arsenal with the help of his knights; Catarina places herself at the head of the Cypriots, who quickly rally to her support. Venice is defeated, and the dying king places the fateful crown in his wife's hands. She holds up her little son, who, notwithstanding M. de Saint-Georges' well-meant effort to shorten the time lapse, reveals himself—with strict historical accuracy—as a lusty youngster of at least three years. The people avow their loyalty, and the hospitaller of the Knights of Malta, true to the oath of his order, takes leave of his former sweetheart for ever.

Now who will deny that this is a libretto as good in its way as any one could ever hope to find? It is full of action which, act by act, grips, excites and entertains—touching when it should be and terrifying when terror is called for; it offers the composer all sorts of opportunities to display his talents and skills.

Yet all the same it would never occur to anybody to call this libretto a work of art. Above all, the author has most decidedly shown himself to be devoid of the gift we call *poetry:* there is nothing in his work that suggests some higher spiritual idea; no inner impulse has gripped him; no burning enthusiasm carried him away. He has simply seized on the first historical fact that offered itself. With no thought of any particular underlying idea, he chose this story either merely because he did not happen to find another, or because his experience told him that in adapting it he could employ all those popular and gripping effects which are the stock in trade of Parisian librettists, used successfully by all of them time and time again. This is evident throughout the opera: every scene is interesting and entertaining, but nothing brings us even for a moment to a pitch of real enthusiasm or sets our higher thoughts in motion. However, M. de Saint-Georges is astute enough to know that now and again a touch of enthusiasm must be introduced. In *La Reine de Chypre* as elsewhere he has not neglected to win the hearts of the audience through an appeal to its sympathy. Here he utilises the fact that Gerard and Lusignan, who meet adventurously in Cyprus, are both of them Frenchmen, to make them burst out in rhapsodies about the 'lovely land of France'. He knows that this cannot fail of effect, since Paris audiences consist for the greater part of French people. And there is the additional advantage that this scene can easily be adapted to suit the patriotic feelings of any nation. If the opera were being presented in Munich, for example, one would only have to change Venice into Russia, Cyprus into Greece, call Lusignan King Otto and turn Gerard into a retired Bavarian cavalry officer, and then that duet could be sung quite happily to the words 'Hail, thou lovely land of Bavaria', which could not fail to arouse enthusiasm. I shall be curious to see whether M. de Saint-Georges has not done precisely this in his libretto for Lachner's opera *Catarina Cornaro*.

So you see, my dear German opera librettists, how easy it is to discover truly excellent subjects, to stuff them full of interesting happenings and even to conjure up a semblance of enthusiasm without putting yourselves to any more trouble than it costs to acquire a certain measure of skill. You have the additional advantage over the French that you are far less restricted by censorship problems. You can safely allow Venetian conspiracies to break out in Cyprus, for example, whereas here there have been great difficulties, since the French government feared the conspiracies might be taken to refer to the recent risings in Toulouse. But, leaving that aside, you see that you have only to choose some historical occasion or other and to trick it out with all sorts of family and social events such as weddings, elopements, duels and so on, and you will provide some talented composer with sufficient opportunity to display his dramatic skill in a thousand brilliant ways and keep any audience thoroughly entertained for four or five hours.

M. Halévy has fully succeeded in doing this. His music is appropriate, full of feeling and in some places even impressive in effect. Gracefulness, which I had not previously noted among Halévy's talents, is apparent in the many opportunities for song that the libretto so richly provides, and above all I was struck by a welcome tendency towards simplicity in the treatment as a whole. It would be of great significance for our time if this tendency were to be fostered by the Paris Opéra at a period in which our German opera composers have just begun to imitate French luxury and pomp: we should then need to do no more than turn back on our tracks half-way in order to beat the French to this backward-looking goal. However, Halévy's efforts to achieve simplicity have been successful only in his writing for the voice, from which he has banished all those baleful acrobatics and insufferable prima donna flourishes which (admittedly much to the enjoyment of the illustrious Parisian dilettantes) have crept into the pen of many a bright composer of French operas from the scores of Donizetti and his like. Halévy's handling of the orchestra has on the other hand turned out much less well. If we are to give up the modern way of using the brass instruments (though God knows why we should), we should also by rights have to abandon the style of composition which called for it. But the conception of dramatic music peculiar (for instance) to Halévy can in truth be regarded as a step forward rather than a step back, and what I might call its inherent *historical* tendency should provide a good basis on which to build further and to solve problems which have perhaps not yet even been posed. It cannot be disputed that an intelligent use of the brass instruments, such as Halévy shows in *La Juive*, is of true historical significance. Should this talented composer now have allowed himself to be frightened off using them—perhaps because he has seen how frightfully this style of instrumentation has been misused by the more modern Italian opera-makers and by Parisian quadrille composers—then not only is he committing a grave error, but he is also doing damage to his own style of composition. For, I repeat, in this opera, his most recent work, he has not abandoned his previous conception of dramatic music: in the first two acts one finds passages of a character demanding a completely different, I would say more 'modern' instrumentation to obtain the desired effect. Halévy has made the mistake of asking clarinets and oboes, for example, to provide effects which can only be expected from horns and valve-trumpets, and so these passages give the impression of having been orchestrated by an inexperienced beginner. In the course of the opera the composer fortunately drops his inhibitions and orchestrates as his true nature dictates. Apart from this—and it is after all a secondary matter—the last acts are more effective than the opening ones. Moments of great beauty are to be found in every number, and particular mention must be made of the last act, to which the composer, as distinct from the librettist, has managed to impart a truly poetic flavour. The dying king becomes a moving and significant figure, and the quartet arising from the situation which I called electrifying in my description of the libretto makes a truly shattering effect. A certain awesome grandeur, tinged with an elegiac flavour, is always a characteristic feature of Halévy's best and most heart-felt productions.

To sum up, therefore, I might say that, if this work does not reach the heights of *La Juive*, the fault is not due to any decline in the composer's creative powers, but rather to the lack of a compelling overall poetic quality in the libretto, such as was undoubtedly present in *La Juive*. All the same, the Paris Opéra can be congratulated on the birth of this new work for it is decidedly the best that has appeared on its boards since Meyerbeer's *Hugeunots*.

And you, my illustrious fifty-two German opera directors, you can be happy too, for you have once more been presented with a new child, without having yourselves to suffer a single twinge of labour pains! Should the time ever come when you will be obliged to stretch out loving arms to receive healthy German babies, do not be angry with me for having brought them into existence. For though I cannot doubt that the discoveries and helpful hints contained in this essay concerning the craft of libretto-writing will at once inspire our German dramatists to produce the best stories in the world for our composers, my motive was not to deprive you of property and fortune, but rather a wild hope that I might be pointing out to you an even more glorious source of profit. Of this you can be assured.

Paris, 31 December 1841.

A Happy Evening

It was a lovely evening in spring. Already the heat of summer could be felt in the currents of warm air which at every breath stirred and enchanted us as though they were sighs of passionate love. We were following the crowd which was pouring into the public gardens: an orchestra was opening the series of concerts which it gave there every summer. There was a festival atmosphere. My good friend R— was in raptures. (He had not yet taken that fatal trip of his to Paris.) Already before the commencement of the concert he was intoxicated with music; this, he declared, was the inner music which always resounded through him when the evening was a lovely one in spring and he felt happy.

We arrived and took our usual place at a table under a large oak tree, a place at the furthest possible distance from the idle crowd and which we knew from experience had the particular merit of being the one where the music could be most distinctly heard. We always pitied those unfortunates who at every concert, whether in gardens or in salons, felt themselves obliged, or indeed preferred, to sit right close to the orchestra. We found it impossible to understand how they could enjoy *looking* at music instead of listening to it. We presumed that this must be so, since how otherwise could one explain their intense concentration upon the musicians' various physical movements, in particular their ardent interest in the percussion player anxiously counting his rests before coming in with his thunderous contribution. We were agreed that when a beautiful instrumental piece is being performed nothing is more prosaic and off-putting than the spectacle of the wind player's horribly swollen cheeks and distorted physiognomy, than the unaesthetic scrabbling of the double basses and cellos, than the boring up-and-down movements of the violinists' bows. Therefore we had chosen a place from which we could hear the orchestra's every nuance without being distracted by the sight of the players.

The concert began. Many beautiful things were played, among them Mozart's Symphony in E flat and Beethoven's in A.

The concert came to an end. My friend sat opposite me, his arms crossed, saying nothing but smiling happily. The rustling crowd moved off gradually; here and there a few tables were still occupied. The balmy warmth of the evening began to give way to the chill of night.

'Let's have a glass of punch!' cried R—, changing his position and looking round for a waiter.

A mood such as that into which we had been thrown is so holy that one is bound to seek to prolong it as long as possible. Since I knew how the enjoyment of a glass of punch would serve that purpose, I gladly supported my friend's proposal. Soon a not insubstantial bowl was steaming on the table and we emptied our first glass.

'How did you like the performance of the symphonies?' I asked.

'Oh, bother the performance!' R— replied. 'However exacting I am normally, in some moods I am capable of being enchanted by the very worst performance of a favourite work. Such moods are rare, of course: they only possess me when my whole inner being is in harmony with my bodily state. Then I only need to be faintly reminded of a work corresponding to the mood, and I hear the whole of it complete in my mind, and in a performance so perfect that the best orchestra in the world could never equal it. My rigorous ear becomes so pliable that I only wince very slightly when the oboist misses a note; even the wrong note of a trumpet I let pass with a considerate smile in order that my bliss should not be disturbed and I can continue to enjoy the flattering illusion that I am hearing the perfect performance of my favourite work. In such moods nothing annoys me so much as to have to listen to some smooth-eared fop complaining with a fine show of cultured indignation at some lapse which has offended his delicate hearing—though this does not prevent him the next day admiring some favourite prima donna or other who lacerates our nerves and our souls with the piercing shrillness of her vocal acrobatics. Music never gets past the ears of these clever fools; indeed often never past the eyes: I remember noticing people who never moved a muscle when a wind instrument made a wrong entry yet immediately put their hands to their ears when they saw the worthy player shaking his head in shame and confusion!'

'What a surprise to hear you of all people railing against people with sensitive ears!' I interjected. 'How often have I not seen you driven to madness by the faulty intonation of a singer!'

'Oh my friend!' cried R—,'I am speaking only of how I feel now, today. God knows how often I have been maddened by the intonation of the most famous violinist, how often I have cursed the most famous prima donna when she imagines her do-re-mis are at their purest, indeed how often I have been unable to find the slightest harmonic accord between the instruments of the most carefully tuned orchestra! This, you see, is how I feel on those countless days when my good angel deserts me and I put on my evening dress and go off with perfumed ladies and coiffeured gentlemen to seek refreshment for my soul through my ears. You cannot imagine how anxiously I weigh every tone and measure every vibration! When my heart is not touched I can be every bit as clever as the fools who annoyed me today, and there have been times when even a Beethoven violin or cello sonata could put me to flight. . . . But today—praise be to God, who created the season of spring and the art of music!—today I am happy and can tell you that I am!' So saying he filled our glasses again and we drained them to the last drop.

'For my part, I feel no less happy,' I began. 'How could it be otherwise when one has just been listening in calm and comfort to two works which seem to have been created by the god of an exalted contemplative joy? I found the juxtaposition of the Mozart and Beethoven symphonies very apt: I felt I had discerned some wonderful affinity between the two: both express a clear human consciousness of happiness as the goal of existence, and in both this expression is beautifully and revealingly interwoven with a sense of something higher beyond this earth. I would make the distinction, though, that in Mozart's music the language of the heart is formulated as a graceful longing, whereas in Beethoven's the longing is a daring, high-spirited endeavour to grasp the infinite. Mozart's symphony is dominated by awareness of sensibility, Beethoven's by a bold consciousness of strength.'

'It always delights me,' my friend replied, 'to hear views of that sort expressed about the nature and significance of exalted instrumental works. Not that I think that those few sentences of yours, thrown out on the spur of the moment, get to the bottom of the matter: to understand such creations, let alone formulate the understanding, lies outside the scope of speech, just as it lies outside the scope of music to express what only words, the organ of the poet, can convey. It is a pity that so many people go to the unnecessary trouble of mixing the languages of music and poetry in order that the one might provide a supplement or substitute for what according to their limited ideas is deficient in the other. It is an eternal truth that music begins where speech ends. Nothing is so intolerable as those tasteless pictures and stories with which some people try to buttress instrumental works. What poverty of intellect and sensibility is revealed by people who can only manage to maintain their interest in a Beethoven symphony by imagining that the stream of music represents the plot of some novel or other. Then they complain when some unexpected stroke of the master upsets the orderly development of the supposed story; they say he is obscure and confused and deplore his lack of continuity—Oh, what fools!'

'Let them be,' I replied. 'Let each according to his imaginative capacity help himself out with stories and pictures if that is the only way he can get pleasure from great musical revelations; without such an aid many would get none at all. At least you must admit that it is in this way that our Beethoven's following has increased so greatly, and indeed it can surely be hoped that the works of the great master will achieve a popularity such as they could never have enjoyed if they could only be understood in an ideal sense.'

'Oh for heaven's sake!' cried R—. 'Must these holy works be saddled with the banal popularity which is the curse of everything noble and glorious? Is that what you want? Are *they* honoured when their rousing rhythms—their temporal framework—are danced to in a village inn?'

'You exaggerate!' I answered evenly. 'It is not a popularity of the street and village inn that I demand for the symphonies of Beethoven. Even so, if these works are able to quicken the sluggish blood of ordinary small-minded folk surely this should be regarded as a proof of their merit?'

'These symphonies don't require any such proof!' my friend retorted angrily. 'They are there for their own sake, not to set the blood of some philistine into circulation. Let him who can acquire the merit of grasping them: they themselves are under no obligation to force themselves upon the understanding of cold hearts!'

I filled our glasses and said, smiling: 'The same old fantasist, so carried away that you misunderstand me when really we are of the same opinion. Let us leave aside the question of popularity. Instead, give me the pleasure of hearing an account of your feelings as you listened to those two symphonies just now.'

My friend's face, which had been clouded by the annoyance of his recent outburst, cleared. 'My feelings? . . . I felt the balmy warmth of a lovely spring evening and imagined that I was sitting with you under a big oak tree and gazing up at the starry sky through its branches. And I felt a thousand other things of which I cannot speak. There you have it!'

'Not bad,' I answered. 'Perhaps one of our neighbours imagined that he was smoking a cigar, drinking coffee and making eyes at a young lady in blue.'

'No doubt,' R—continued sarcastically, 'and perhaps the drummer imagined that he was beating his naughty children for not having brought him his evening sandwich from town. . . . Splendid! At the entrance of the garden I saw a peasant listening to the A major Symphony with joy and wonder written all over his face; I'll wager my head he had the right idea: according to a recent article in one of our musical journals, which you must have read, Beethoven's intention when he composed this symphony was to depict a peasants' wedding; just that and nothing else. That honest countryman must have been reminded of his wedding day. He was reliving the whole sequence: the arrival of the guests; the wedding feast; the procession to the church; the blessing; then the dance; and finally the best of all, which bride and bridegroom keep to themselves.'

'A good idea!' I exclaimed laughing. 'But tell me for heaven's sake why you scout the idea of this symphony providing that worthy peasant with an hour of happiness such as he can enjoy in his way? Was he not relatively experiencing the same delight which you felt when you sat under the oak tree and gazed up at the stars through its branches?'

'I concede the point,' my friend replied good-humouredly; 'and with pleasure allow the good peasant to be reminded by the A major Symphony of his wedding day. But I would like to tear the hair from the silly heads of the sophisticated townsfolk who write for musical journals and spread stupid nonsense which prevents honest people from listening to a Beethoven symphony simply and naturally without any preconceptions, as otherwise they would do. Instead of relying upon their own spontaneous impressions, warm-hearted weak-headed people are led to suppose that they must picture a peasants' wedding which probably they have never attended, whereas left to themselves they would certainly have much preferred to picture something within the field of their own imagination.'

'You admit then', I replied, 'that such works are capable of being conceived in different ways by different individuals?'

'Certainly I do', ran the reply. 'To my mind the idea of a single stereotyped conception is completely inadmissible. However finished and rounded the proportions of the purely musical structure of a Beethoven symphony, however perfect and indivisible in a higher sense such a work may be, it does not follow that its imprint on the heart of the listener is a uniform one. The same is more or less true of the other arts: think how differently a picture or drama can affect different individuals; and for that matter a single individual at different times! And this notwithstanding the fact that painters and poets, drawing as they do their stuff from the appearances of everyday life, are bound to shape their works more definitely and specifically than the instrumental composer, whose sphere is the immeasurable realm of the unearthly, and whose medium that most immaterial of all stuffs, tone. One is dragging the musician down from his lofty position when one demands that he suit his inspiration to the appearances of everyday life. And the instrumental composer would be betraying his mission and exposing his weaknesses were to he attempt to transfer the limited proportions of worldly appearances into the sphere of his own art.'

'You condemn tone-painting, then?' I asked.

'In every case,' R— replied, 'except when it is employed for comic effect or when it is a question of reproducing some purely musical phenomenon. In a joke everything is allowed, its essence is a certain deliberately assumed narrowness, and anyway to laugh and make others laugh is a fine thing. But tone-painting is absurd when it goes beyond this. The impulses and inspirations behind an instrumental composition must be of a kind which could only originate in the soul of a musician!'

'There you are saying something which you would find hard to prove,' I answered. 'At bottom I am of the same opinion, but I doubt whether it can be completely reconciled with our mutual reverence for the works of the great master. Don't you yourself feel that your statement doesn't fully coincide with Beethoven's own revelations?'

'Not in the least; on the contrary it is upon Beethoven that I base my case.'

'Before we go into details,' I continued, 'let me ask whether you wouldn't agree that Mozart's conception of instrumental music bears out your contention far more closely than Beethoven's?'

'Not that I know of,' my friend replied. 'Beethoven infinitely expanded the form of the symphony. He discarded the proportions of the traditional periodic structure, wrought to their highest beauty by Mozart, in order that his turbulent, daring, and yet at the same time reflective, genius might be free to take wing in realms to which it alone could penetrate. Nevertheless, since he knew how to impart a philosophic consistency to those daring flights of his, it is undeniable that Beethoven created a completely new genre on the basis of the Mozart symphony, and that he perfected this genre and raised it to a solitary supreme height. All this he could never have achieved if Mozart had not already applied his victorious genius to the symphony, if Mozart's vitalising, idealising breath had not already imparted spiritual warmth to its arid forms and proportions. Mozart was Beethoven's point of departure; he absorbed Mozart's divinely pure spirit; thereafter he could never descend from the elevated sphere which is the realm of true music.'

'You are right,' I rejoined. 'Nevertheless you can hardly deny that Mozart's inspirations flow from a source of pure music; that they are bound up with indefinite feelings which, even if he had had the ability of a poet, could never have been formulated in words, but only in tones. I am thinking especially of the inspirations which occur to a composer *together with* melodies and tonal forms; such inspirations are written all over Mozart's music; so much so that it is impossible to imagine him writing a symphony of which he did not already have in his head every theme, indeed the whole design, exactly as we know it. In the case of Beethoven, on the other hand, I find it hard not to imagine that a symphony was planned in advance in accordance with some specific philosophic idea, and that he then left it to his musical imagination to invent the themes.'

'On which of his works would you demonstrate that?' my friend interjected swiftly. 'On the symphony we have just been listening to?'

'It would be difficult to do so there,' I answered. 'But surely the very name of the "Eroica" Symphony speaks for itself. You know that the symphony was originally intended to bear the title of "Bonaparte". How can you deny that Beethoven was inspired by an idea outside the realm of music, and that it was this which determined the plan of that gigantic work?'

'I'm glad you mentioned that symphony,' R— replied quickly. 'Tell me—do you think that the idea of heroic strength striving titanically for a noble cause lies outside the realm of music? Or do you find that Beethoven in this symphony expressed his enthusiasm for the godlike young victor, Bonaparte, in such graphic detail that you could suppose he was intending to write a military account in music of the first Italian campaign?'

'What are you driving at?' I exclaimed. 'I never said anything of that sort!'

'But you implied it,' my friend went on passionately. 'To assume that Beethoven sat down to write a composition in honour of Bonaparte is to imply that he was merely turning out one of those commissioned occasional pieces which are invariably stillborn. But the "Eroica" Symphony flies in the face of such an assumption! One can only say that if *that* had been the master's intention then he carried it out very unsatisfactorily. Can you point to a single passage that could be taken to describe an event in the young general's career? Why the Funeral March, why the Scherzo with hunting horns, why the Finale with its interwoven meltingly expressive Andante? Where is the bridge of Lodi, the battle of Arcola, the march on Leoben, the

victory of the Pyramids, the 18th Brumaire? Surely in this age no
composer of a biographical symphony of Bonaparte would have overlooked any of those things? . . . The truth of the matter is very
different—let me tell you my view of how Beethoven conceived the
symphony. When a musician is moved to sketch out a composition,
no matter how small, he is acting under the influence of a feeling
which in the hour of conception dominates his entire being. The feeling may have been occasioned by some external event or it may have
sprung from some mysterious inner source. Though it may manifest
itself as melancholy, joy, longing, contentment, love or hate nevertheless in the mind of the musician the feeling always takes a musical
form and expresses itself in tones before it has been cast into notes.
Profound, passionate feelings which hold sway over our emotions and
ideas for months and years are the ones which impel the musician to
those broad, all-embracing conceptions to which, among other works,
we owe the existence of the "Eroica". Profound feelings of suffering
or elation may be occasioned by external events since we are human
beings whose destinies in the nature of the case are governed by
extraneous circumstances; but such feelings, when they impel the
musician to create, have already been transmuted into music. Thus
in the moment of creative inspiration the determining factor is no
longer the external event, but the musical feeling which it engen-
dered. . . . What more likely to grip the imagination of a fiery
genius such as Beethoven than the spectacle of the young demi-god,
Bonaparte, destroying the world in order to raise a new one upon its
ruins? What must the heroic musician have felt as he followed the
triumphs of that career which commanded the admiration of friend
and foe alike! Remember too that Beethoven was a republican in
whose eyes the destiny of every hero was to realise the dream of an
ideal universal happiness. What it must have meant to the genius
consulting his muse to hear that resounding name wherever he went!
How it must have quickened his blood and caused his heart to glow!
His strength was challenged, *his* victorious spirit spurred to accomplish something great and unheard of! He was not a general—he was
a musician and on his own territory he could achieve what Bonaparte
had achieved on the fields of Italy. So, his musical powers stretched
to their utmost, Beethoven conceived a work such as had never

before been contemplated, let alone carried out. He wrote the "Eroica" Symphony and knowing to whom he owed the impulse behind his mighty work wrote the name of Bonaparte upon its title page. And indeed is it not true that this symphony is just as great a testimony to man's creative power as Bonaparte's glorious victory? Nevertheless does it possess a single feature directly bearing upon the career of the hero, who at that time had not even reached the pinnacle of his glory? For my part I am content to admire it as a gigantic monument of art, and to be strengthened by the exaltation I feel whenever I hear it. I leave to others, more learned, the task of deciphering the battles of Rivoli and Marengo from the secret hieroglyphics of the score.'

The night air had grown still colder; the waiter, who had approached us during our conversation, had understood my nod and removed the punch in order to heat it up. Now he came back, and once again the warming drink was steaming before our eyes. I drained my glass and stretched out my hand to R—.

'We agree,' I said, 'as we always do whenever we touch upon the deepest questions of art. Were we to accept those crude fallacies you have been denouncing then, simply for that reason, we would be forfeiting the right to call ourselves true musicians, however feeble our talents. What music expresses is eternal, infinite and ideal. It speaks not of the passion, love and longing of this or that individual in this or that situation, but of passion, love and longing in themselves, and furthermore in all the infinite variety of motivations which arise from the exclusive nature of music and which are strange to, and beyond the expression of, every other form of language. Let each according to his strength, his capacity and his disposition take from it what he is capable of feeling and enjoying!'

'Let me tell you what I am feeling,' my friend broke in enthusiastically, 'let me tell you what I am feeling after listening to those revelations of Mozart and Beethoven this glorious spring evening. I feel joyful, I feel happy, I feel enraptured by the intimation of a higher destiny. I want to sing the praises of joy and happiness—and of courage, which steels us to struggle against our fate—and of victory, through which we attain a higher awareness of the triviality of common things—and of love, which rewards courage—and of friendship, which maintains faith—and of hope, which marries itself to our dreams. I want to hail the day and the night and the sun and the stars. And not once but three times I want to hail music and her high priests. Let God, say I, be eternally praised, the God of joy and happiness who created music! . . . Amen.'

Arm in arm we made our way home. We pressed each other by the hand but spoke not a word more.

Index and Notes

ADAM, Adolphe Charles (1803–56)
158–9
French composer of thirty-nine operas,
including the popular *Le Postillon de
Longjumeau*, and fourteen ballets, of
which *Giselle, ou Les Willis* was one.

ANDERS, E. G. 12, 127–8
Described by Wagner in his autobiography as a bachelor in his fifties, son
of a noble Rhineland family. Anders
was not his real name, which he never
revealed. He and Wagner planned to
collaborate on a biography of Beethoven, but it never materialised.

AUBER, Daniel François (1782–1871)
49, 111, 114, 122, 123, 130, 136
La Muette de Portici (also known as
Masaniello) first appeared in 1828. It
was the eighth of a long series of
operas (including *Les Diamants de la
Couronne*) to texts by Scribe, and it
had a huge contemporary impact—
among other things sparking off the
Belgian revolt of 1830. Wagner, who
used sometimes to meet Auber over
ices in a Paris coffee-house, was not
alone in deploring the French composer's later capitulation to easy success.

BERLIOZ, Hector (1803–69) 13, 15,
107, 129–34, 141–2, 143, 147, 152, 157
Like Wagner, Berlioz was a contribu-
tor to the *Gazette musicale*, and they
frequently met in Schlesinger's office
and at his concerts. Neither at that
time nor later did they manage to
achieve a really friendly relationship:
each was fascinated by the music of
the other, but it was an unwilling
fascination, based on no true understanding.

BOIELDIEU, François Adrien (1775–
1834) 49, 114
One of the founders of the French Opéra
comique, he wrote thirty-eight operas
in the years 1793–1831, of which the
best-known are *Jean de Paris* (1812)
and *La Dame blanche* (1825).

BULL, Ole (1810–80) 125
Norwegian violinist, who first appeared in Paris in 1832 and subsequently made tours throughout Europe
and America. His compositions were
purely vehicles for his own virtuosity.

CHERUBINI, Maria Luigi (1760–
1842) 131–2, 134
Influential as he had been as a com-
poser in reforming French opera and
highly respected as director of the
Conservatoire, he had little popular
success in Paris with his operas, which
include *Medea* (1797) and *The Water
Carrier* (1800). His successor at the
Conservatoire in 1842 was not, as
Wagner forecast, Habeneck, but
Auber.

to Paris in performances which Wagner greeted as a revelation. Not he, but Auber, succeeded Cherubini as director of the Conservatoire.

HALÉVY, Jacques Fromental (1799–1862) 12, 111, 113, 114, 122–3, 163–78 *passim*
Wagner's admiration for the French Jewish composer's masterpiece *La Juive* (1835) was lifelong, and he also had a warm personal regard for the man. In a letter to Schumann in February 1842 he remarked: 'He is open and honest—not a deliberate artful dodger like Meyerbeer.' Possibly it was this personal liking that saved Halévy from being castigated in Wagner's essay on music and the Jews—or Wagner's wish conveniently to forget his argument (in *Farewell Performances*) that the strength of *La Juive* owed much to the composer's 'mixed blood'! *La Reine de Chypre* (referred to in the same piece under the title of *Le Chevalier de Malte*) was a considerable success in Paris. It was also produced in German at Leipzig and in Italian at Florence in 1842 and played (in French) in London and New York in 1845.

HEINE, Heinrich (1797–1856) 13, 15, 158, 161–2
Settled in Paris in 1831, from where he wrote reports for the *Allgemeine Zeitung* in Augsburg on the Paris scene (including music).

HEINEFETTER, Kathinka (1820–58) 135
German soprano, one of six sisters, all of whom were opera singers.

HÉROLD, Louis Joseph Ferdinand 1791–1833) 114

One of the founders of the French operatic school, his work was not as despised in Paris as Wagner makes out: both *Zampa* (1831) and *Le Pré aux Clercs* (1832) were permanent successes, while his ballet *La Fille mal gardée* is still frequently played.

ISOUARD, Niccolò (1775–1818) 134
Boieldieu's main rival at the Opéra comique, he achieved wide success throughout Europe, particularly with *Cendrillon* (1810) and *Joconde* (1814).

JANIN, Jules (1804–74) 113, 152
As chief dramatic critic of the *Journal des Débats* an influential figure in Paris.

KASTNER, Johann Georg (1810–67) 159–60
Alsatian composer and theorist whose textbooks were used by the Conservatoire. His compositions include eight operas, of which *La Maschera* (libretto by de Wailly and Arnould) was in fact the sixth.

LABLACHE, Luigi (1794–1858) 12, 58, 59–62, 114–15
Born of French and Irish parents and trained in Italy, he sang regularly in both Paris and London from 1830 onwards (besides giving Queen Victoria singing lessons). A renowned Loporello and Donizetti's first Don Pasquale.

LACHNER, Franz (1803–90) 166, 174
Long-reigning conductor at Munich from 1836 to his death and a prolific composer. *Catarina Cornaro* (1841), his most successful opera, had the same libretto (translated into German) as Halévy's *La Reine de Chypre*, the librettist (Saint-Georges) having sold it to both composers simultaneously.

LISZT, Franz (1811–86) 13, 34, 54–5 (not named), 124–5, 133–4

In 1841 Liszt was at the height of his career as a piano virtuoso. Wagner met him in Paris, but did not like him personally, and it was not until Liszt moved to Weimar as a conductor, presenting *Tannhäuser* there in 1849 and giving the first performance of *Lohengrin* in 1850, that they became friends.

LÖWE, Johanna Sophie (1816-66) 112-13, 115, 135-6
Had great success in Berlin in *Robert le Diable* and *La Sonnambula*. Appeared in London in 1841 in Bellini's *La Straniera*. Failing to obtain a Paris engagement, she returned to Berlin.

MARS, Mlle (1779-1847) 118
French actress particularly renowned in comedy. The evening of which Wagner writes was indeed her final farewell after a career at the Comédie française going back to 1799.

MARSCHNER, Heinrich (1795-1861) 48
Remembered today mainly for *Hans Heiling* (1833), he was (together with Weber, his colleague at Dresden) one of the founders of German romantic opera. Wagner, who as a boy had met him, honoured him by directing the first performance of his *Kaiser Adolf von Nassau* in Dresden in 1845.

MEYERBEER, Giacomo (1791-1864) 11, 12, 14, 32, 50, 107, 111-12, 176
Son of a rich German Jewish banker, his great success in Paris was established with *Robert le Diable* (1831) and *Les Huguenots* (1836). Wagner's ambivalent attitude towards him is reflected in a letter which he wrote to Schumann on 29 December 1840: 'Do please stop pulling Meyerbeer to pieces: I owe the man everything, including my very imminent fame.' Yet Wagner himself could never resist making sly digs in his writings at the 'banker-composer'. It obviously hurt him to be dependent for favours on a man whose work was the antithesis of everything his own art stood for, and the imperturbable charm with which Meyerbeer dispensed these favours (which included recommending *Rienzi* to Dresden and *The Flying Dutchman* to Berlin) only added to the pent-up gall which Wagner released in violent attacks against Meyerbeer in his later writings.

MONPOU, Hippolyte (1804-41) 113
Organist and composer of about ten operas, which enjoyed scant success.

MUSARD, Philippe (1793-1859) 88, 97, 116, 129
Violinist who appeared as leader of dance-concerts and balls in Paris and London. He enjoyed great success as conductor of his own orchestra at 'promenade concerts' and as composer of quadrilles and galops.

PACINI, Emiliano (1811-98) 140-1
Translated Verdi's *Il Trovatore* and *Luisa Miller* as well as *Der Freischütz* for the Opéra and also wrote librettos for some now forgotten operas.

PAGANINI, Niccolò (1782-1840) 107, 130
Following a concert in Paris in 1838, in which Berlioz conducted the *Fantastic Symphony* and *Harold in Italy*, the great Italian violinist sent the composer a letter comparing him with Beethoven and enclosing a gift of 20,000 francs.

PERSIANI, Fanny (1812-67) 59, 113

Italian baritone who sang regularly in Paris and London from 1832. The first Riccardo in *I Puritani* and Malatesta in *Don Pasquale*.

THIERS, Louis Adolphe (1797–1877) 110
March–October 1840 president of the council and foreign minister, but forced to resign when his Egyptian policy threatened to lead to war with Britain.

THOMAS, Ambroise (1811–96) 113, 135
Le Comte de Carmagnola was Thomas's fifth opera and the first at the Opéra, the others being presented at the Opéra comique. He did not achieve real success before *Mignon* in 1866.

VÉRON, Louis Désiré (1798–1867) 119–20
Director of the Opéra from 1831 to 1836.

VIEUXTEMPS, Henri (1820–81) 115–16, 125–6
In fact he first appeared in Paris at the age of ten. Though primarily a virtuoso violinist, he wrote a number of compositions, including six violin concertos. Wagner is here writing about No 1 in E Major. The two men were already friends, having met two years earlier in Riga.

WEBER, Carl Maria von (1786–1826) 48, 138–58 *passim*
During Wagner's boyhood Weber was conductor of the Dresden Opera and an occasional visitor in Wagner's home, being interested in the singing talents of his sister Klara. He writes in his autobiography of the fascination of Weber's 'delicate, suffering, spiritualised appearance'. *Der Freischütz*, which Wagner first saw in Dresden as a young boy, made an indelible impression on him even before he could really understand it. After himself taking over Weber's old position at Dresden, Wagner arranged in 1844 for the reburial there of Weber's ashes, brought from London. 'Never,' he said in his funeral oration, 'has a more truly German musician ever lived.' See also entry under *Robin des Bois*.

WEIGL, Joseph (1766–1846) 47
Austrian composer of more than thirty operas, of which *Die Schweizerfamilie* (The Swiss Family, 1809) was the most successful. For a production of it in Riga Wagner composed an insertion 'which really pleased even myself'.

WINTER, Peter von (1754–1825) 47
Wrote some forty operas, of which three were first produced in London, other in Milan and Paris. *Das unterbrochene Opferfest* (The Interrupted Sacrifice, 1796) was the most successful.

Wagner's Writings in Paris

The pieces marked with an asterisk were omitted by Wagner from his own edition of the collected writings, of which the first nine volumes were published in 1871 and the tenth in 1885, two years after his death They were included in the second of two supplementary volumes which his publishers, E. W. Fritzsch of Leipzig, added to their fourth edition in 1907. All save one insignificant piece are to be found in the eighth volume of the English translation of the collected writings made (1892–9) by W. Ashton Ellis. In that volume and in the seventh volume (containing all of the pieces which Wagner himself included in his collected writings) the reader will also find a wealth of scholarly annotation, to which we take this opportunity of acknowledging our debt.

Title	Periodical	Publication date
		1840
German Music (*Über deutsches Musikwesen*)	*Gazette musicale*	July (12, 26)
* *Pergolesi's Stabat Mater*	*Gazette musicale*	October (11)
The Virtuoso and the Artist (*Der Virtuos und der Künstler*)	*Gazette musicale*	October (18)
A Pilgrimage to Beethoven (*Eine Pilgerfahrt zu Beethoven*)	*Gazette musicale*	November (19, 22, 29), December (3)
		1841
The Overture (*Über die Ouvertüre*)	*Gazette musicale*	January (10, 14, 17)
Death in Paris (*Ein Ende in Paris*)	*Gazette musicale*	January (31), February (7, 11)
* Report from Paris I: The Opéra Lies Dying (*Pariser Berichte I*)	*Abendzeitung*, Dresden	March (19, 20, 22)
The Artist and the Public (*Der Künstler und die Öffentlichkeit*)	*Gazette musicale*	April (1)

Der Freischütz in Paris (*Der Freischütz. An das Pariser Publikum*)	*Gazette musicale*	May (23, 30)
* Report from Paris II: Farewell Performances (*Pariser Berichte II*)	*Abendzeitung,* Dresden	May (24, 28)
* Report from Paris III: Berlioz and Liszt (*Pariser Berichte III*)	*Abendzeitung,* Dresden	June (14, 17)
* Traps for Unwary Germans in Paris (*Pariser Fatalitäten für Deutsche*)	*Europa*	Third quarter
Le Freischutz	*Abendzeitung,* Dresden	July (16, 21)
* Report from Paris IV: Wonders from Abroad (*Pariser Berichte IV*)	*Abendzeitung,* Dresden	August (2, 4)
* Report from Paris V (*Pariser Berichte V*)	*Abendzeitung,* Dresden	August (28)
* Paris Amusements (*Pariser Amüsements*)	*Europa*	Fourth quarter
* Report from Paris VI (*Pariser Berichte VI*)	*Abendzeitung,* Dresden	October (1, 2)
A Happy Evening (*Ein glücklicher Abend*)	*Gazette musicale*	October (24), November (27)
* Report from Paris VII (*Pariser Berichte VII*)	*Abendzeitung,* Dresden	December (4, 8)
* Report from Paris VIII (*Pariser Berichte VIII*)	*Abendzeitung,* Dresden	December (25)
Rossini's Stabat Mater	*Neue Zeitschrift für Musik*	December (28)
		1842
* Report from Paris IX (*Pariser Berichte IX*)	*Abendzeitung,* Dresden	January (10, 11)
A First Night at the Opéra (*Bericht über eine neue Pariser Oper*)	*Abendzeitung,* Dresden	January (26, 29)
* Report from Paris	*Neue Zeitschrift für Musik*	February (22)
* Halévy's *Reine de Chypre*	*Gazette musicale*	February (27), March (18), April (24), May (1)

BIOGRAPHICAL NOTE

RICHARD WAGNER

born in Leipzig in 1813, was as a boy more interested in drama than in music, but in his late teens, after only six months' study with a good music teacher, he launched out as a composer and conductor. It was not until after the abortive bid for fame in Paris of which this book tells that he achieved success with *Rienzi*, first produced in Dresden in 1842. This was followed by *The Flying Dutchman* (1843), *Tannhäuser* (1845) and *Lohengrin* (1850), and it was these works, performed all over Europe during his lifetime, on which his contemporary fame rested. He had great difficulty in completing and securing productions for the great music dramas which incorporate his revolutionary ideas on opera as set out in his books, *The Art Work of the Future* and *Opera and Drama*, and his second bid to conquer Paris with a revised version of *Tannhäuser* in 1861 led to one of the most spectacular fiascos in operatic history. Eventually, however, he found a friend and supporter in the young King Ludwig II of Bavaria, and he was able to present *Tristan und Isolde* (1865) and *The Mastersingers of Nuremberg* (1868) in Munich, and after that to build his own festival theatre in Bayreuth. There he produced the *Ring* cycle in 1876 (for the first time in its entirety) and *Parsifal*, his last work, in 1882. He died in Venice in 1883.

Wagner's uncompromising ideas did not confine themselves to artistic matters, and his involvement in the 1849 revolution in Saxony put an end to his conducting post in Dresden. After that he spent most of his time in Switzerland until rescued by King Ludwig, living on occasional conducting engagements (including a season with the Royal Philharmonic Society in London in 1855) and loans from friends. His first marriage to Minna Planer, a German actress (1809–66), took place in 1836 and was happy until the Dresden debacle, after which they drew further and further apart. In 1870 Wagner married Liszt's daughter Cosima who, while still married to the conductor Hans von Bülow, bore Wagner two daughters and a son, Siegfried, whose birth inspired the famous *Siegfried Idyll*.